AF657651

Citizenship and Governance

are inhabitants of other city-state. He stipulated that the young and old could not be a citizen for former was immature and the latter infirm. Aristotle pointed out that in order to discharge the functions effectively citizen needed to inhabit a polis that was compact and close-knit.

Aristotle says that the citizen should know both how to rule and how to obey. Citizens are all who share in the civic life of ruling and being ruled in turn. They must possess the knowledge and the capacity requisite for ruling as well as being ruled. Aristotle believed in the dictum that he who has never learnt to obey can not be a good commander. He also considered a good citizen is someone who could live in harmony with the constitution and enough experience, education and leisure time to devote himself to task and responsibilities of active citizenship. A good citizen would possess virtue or moral goodness that would help in realizing a selfless and cooperative civic life.

Roman Theory of Citizenship

Rome developed a pragmatic, flexible and legalistic notion of citizenship. Romans developed a form of citizenship which was more complex, flexible and legalistic. The basic difference from the Greeks was that it was extended to the plebeians, underprivileged aliens domiciled in Rome, traders and merchants. In Rome, citizens enjoyed six privileges:

(a) service in the army;

(b) voting in the assembly;

(c) eligibility to public office;

(d) legal right to action and appeal;

(e) intermarriage; and

(f) trade with other Roman citizens.

In the fourth century, Rome's basic concept of citizenship underwent three historically significant alterations. [illegible] conferred full citizenship on the male members of [illegible] from the region of Latium. The distinction [illegible] and Roman citizenship was also introduced [illegible]

Citizenship and Governance

Dr. Sunita Mangla
Head, Dept of Political Science
Kalindi College, University of Delhi

2015
Kaveri Books
New Delhi - 110 002

First Published in 2015
© Publishers

ISBN: 978-81-7479-168-9

All rights reserved including the right to translate or to reproduce this book or part thereof in any form and through any means except for brief quotations in articles or critical reviews.

Published by
Kaveri Books
4832/24, Ansari Road
New Delhi-110002 (India)
Tel: 011-23288140, 23245799
E-mail : kaveribooks@vsnl.com
kaveribooks@gmail.com
Website: www.kaveribooks.com

Typeset at
Delta Book World, New Delhi - 110 002.

PRINTED IN INDIA

PREFACE

In todays era of globalization, the issue of governance and citizenship have reached at the centre stage of discusssion. We are talking of global governance and global citizenship where National Physical boundaries are loosing their relevance. The purpose of this book is to make students aware of the contemporary global issues of good governance.

1. Objective and Expected Outcome

- To expose the students to some key challenges of contemporary India.
- To enable the students to understand issues of governance in light of these challenges.
- To make them understand, how can the idea of active and participatory citizenship improve the quality of governance?
- The paper will provide the students perspective and insight of governance. It will help them become more informed and effective in their role as citizen.

Every Semester, teaching will be spread over 16 weeks including two weeks for review.

2. Themes & Sub-themes (28 Lectures plus 14 Presentations spread over 14 weeks)

I. The Concept of Good Governance (5 Lectures)

What is Good Governance? Good Governance vs Democratic Governance, Economic Development and Governance, Challenges to Good Governance

II. Citizens and their Rights and Obligations (5 Lectures)

Rights and Obligations of Citizens: Civic Culture, Participatory Citizenship, Social Audit, Citizen Policing, Role of Civil Society

III. Law Enforcement and Administration of Justice (6 Lectures)

Policing and Enforcement of Laws, Autonomy and Neutrality of Investigating and Enforcement Agencies, Access to Justice (Judicial delays, costly litigations etc).

IV. Rural and Urban Governance: Access to Opportunities and Amenities (7 Lectures)

Rural Poverty and Migration to Cities: Issues in Access to Food, Employment, Public Health and Education, Impact of Urbanization on Civic Amenities, Infrastructure and Environment.

V. Institutional Initiatives towards Good Governance (5 Lectures)

Right to Information, Citizen's Charter, Consumer Rights, Indian Ombudsman, E-Governance

Classroom Teaching

- Discussion will be built by connecting the students with the current issues linked to governance.
- Case studies and projects will precede the discussions on theory.
- Focused group discussions on text based materials so as to make classes more interactive and participatory.
- Data Collection through survey methods on several issues pertaining to real world day-to-day problems. This will enable the students to have first-hand access to information and facts which will improve their understanding.

3. Project Works

- Study of efficiency, accountability and transparency in the working of public institutions such as Delhi Jal Board, New Delhi Municipal Corporation, Delhi Electricity Board, etc.
- Study of efficiency, accountability and transparency in the working of public institutions such as Delhi Jal Board, New Delhi Municipal Corporation, Delhi Electricity Board, etc.

- Projects demonstrating as how technology has enabled better governance. Study of People using technology and online access to information, grievance redressal mechanism and delivery system. Projects demonstrating as how technology has enabled better governance. Study of People using technology and online access to information, grievance redressal mechanism and delivery system.
- Case studies on facilities and working of hospitals and schools.
- Projects to assess the correlation between governance and economic development.
- Case study of Government agencies on their service delivery and grievance redressal mechanism.
- Citizens' reactions and responses to national crisis.
- Study of visits of People Representatives to their Constituencies and their interaction with the people.
- Study and analysis of election data to know the linkages between social and religious demography of the constituencies and electoral behaviour.
- Study of educational and professional background of legislators.
- Study of walk-outs and disruptions of legislative proceedings by elected representatives.
- Voting percentage in rural and urban constituencies: Discerning emerging patterns.
- Why corruption cases do not reach the logical end in India?
- Judicial delays and issue of access to justice.
- Workload of civil and police officials.
- Encroachment of public space by citizens.
- Citizens promoting corruption and black money (Survey of consumers and Shopkeepers in buying and selling goods).
- Citizens monitoring/audit of implementation of government programmes and projects.
- Study of Citizens' Charter in public organizations (Banks, Hospitals, Electricity Department, etc),

- Project to study efficiency, accountability and responsiveness of police department.
- Pending court cases: pattern and nature. Projects to assess the workload on judiciary.
- Understanding the nature and pattern of crimes against women.
- Case studies on judicial delays, interaction with litigants and lawyers to study the cost of litigations.
- Studies of perception of people on some high profile corruption and criminal cases.
- Study of traffic violations at red light.
- Filing an RTI application and study of use and misuse of the RTI.
- Evaluation of public protests movements: Analysis of the cost of strike days
- Study of Non-Governmental Organizations (NGOs)to see how they complement the functions of the government.
- Study of protest movements against corruption, black money, land acquisition and displacements, etc.

EDITORIAL

The purpose of the Foundation Course: Governance and Citizenship introduced by University of Delhi is to make students familiar with the contemporary problems and challenges, Indian society is facing today. The Indian society is currently facing plethora of problems like corruption, casetism, communalism, governance deficit, etc. which are threatening its unity and integrity. Being world's largest functioning democracy it has massive responsiblity to empower its citizenry and help them to become informed citizens. Good governance is only possible when both government and citizens take active participation in the public matters and when decision making is made more and more decentralized. Good governance "encompasses the role of public authorities in establishing the environment in which economic operators function and indetermining the distribution of benefits as well as the relationship between the ruler and the ruled." In 1998, the concept of governance was for the first time highlighted in a World Bank document on sub - Saharan Africa. Good-governance meant, at that time as sound development. In this context, World Bank identified four key dimensions, Public Sector Management, Accountability, Legal Framework for Development, Information and Transparency. The purpose of this course is to enable students to understand issues of governance in light of these challenges.

Effective law enforcement and administration of justice is very vital in the sustenance of democratic structures and it lays down the foundation of a stable political system. To provide cheap, quick and accessible justice to its citizenry is the basic responsibility of any nation-state. Delay in delivery of justice generates dissatisfaction among the citizens against the state and its established institutions. Corruption, pendency of cases and costly litigation are biggest challenges in front of Indian citizens and, cheap and quick justice have become a nightmare and "Justice delayed is justice denied"is a stark reality.

The right to citizenship is a vital linchpin in the modern democratic system. A citizen is someone who possesses rights, which are denied to the foreigners. In the liberal theory of citizenship certain rights have been guaranteed by Constitution to be honoured by the state. These are basic rights that allow a person to realize individual growth by way of having access to various facilities and opportunities. The original meaning of the term right stood for a power or privilege as in the right of the nobility, the right of the clergy, and, of course, the divine right of the kings. In its modern sense, it refers to an entitlement to act or to be treated in a particular way. Most modern thinkers have nevertheless been prepared to express their ideas in terms ofrights or entitlements. Marshall divides citizenship rights into three categories: civil rights, political rights and social rights.

In any functioning democratic system the role of civil society can't be undermined. Civil society is a "space" that creates possiblities of communication, interaction and cooperation between the state and the people. These bodies function as mediator between the individual, community and the state distinguishes it from the government and the business sector. The members of the civil society are enlightened and active citizens with a vision to improve the living condition of the people, to help government administer, keep a vigil on the government functionaries, advocate socio-economic growth by promoting education and other citizen related issues.

The book will be immensely useful for students and the general readers who have the interest in the subject matter.

The utmost care has been taken while writing the book, but even if any discrepancy creeps in, needless to say the responsibility would me mine.

Dr. Sunita Mangla

CONTENTS

1

CONCEPT OF GOOD GOVERNANCE

MANILA NARZARY*

When we talk about Governance it does not simply mean rule or administration, it is also about how the power is exercised, decisions are made and implemented. Governance is about the capacity of the public authority and its accountability. Governance can be used in several context such as corporate governance and local governance. Since governance is the process of decision making and how the decisions are implemented, it focuses on the formal and informal actors involved in decision making and implementation of decision properly. (Chakrabarty and Chand, 2012:122)

Governance has become a concept that includes more and more phenomena related to the steering of societal developments. The steering of developments had to be left to societal actors and had to be accomplished through networks in which hierarchy hardly played a role. The term "good governance" is abused by using so many indicators that it becomes nearly impossible to achieve good governance. At the same time, many governments but are also locked in conflicts of interests between trying to do the right things and doing the urgently needed things right. It is not self-evident that improving governance will result in a reduction of the societal and managerial problems. The innovations may provide short term responses to serious

---

* Assistant Professor, Deptt. of Political Science, Kalindi College, Univ. of Delhi

governance deficits, but may not provide long term solutions to them.

The term governance, as generally used, encompasses all aspects of the way country is governed, including its economic policies and regulatory framework. Open democratic and accountable systems of governance, based on respect for human rights and the rule of law, are preconditions for sustainable development and robust growth.

VARYING DEFINITIONS OF GOVERNANCE

According to World Bank's hand book – it is the way "power is exercised through a country's economic, political, and social institutions".

According to UNDP- Governance is "the exercise of economic political and administrative authority to manage a country's affairs at all levels. It comprises mechanism, process and institutions through which citizens and groups articulate their interest, exercises their legal rights, meet their obligations, and mediate their differences".

According to Kaufman- the governance is "the traditions and institutions by which authority in a country is exercised".

DIMENSIONS OF GOVERNANCE

According to World Bank documents governance basically includes:

(a) Voice and accountability, which includes civil liberties and political stability;

(b) Government effectiveness, which includes the quality of policy making and public service delivery;

(c) The quality of regulatory framework;

(d) The rule of law, which includes protection of property rights;

(e) Independence of judiciary;

(f) Cribbing corruption;

"Fundamental aspects of governance" are: graft, rule of law, and the government effectiveness. Other dimensions are voice and accountability, political instability and violence and regulatory burden (Kaufman Kraay and Zoido-Loaton 1999).

Property rights, rule based governance; the quality of budgetary and financial management; the efficiency of revenue mobilization and public expenditure; transparency, accountability and corruption. concerns are some key areas of governance. (World Bank CPIA indicators)

Governance determines who has the power, who takes the decision, how other players make their voices heard and how account is rendered. Ultimately, good governance serves to realize organizational and societal goals.

Governance can be defined as the exercise of political authority and the use of institutional resources to manage problems and the affairs of the society. An alternate definition sees governance as the use of institutions, structures of authority and even collaboration to allocate resources and coordinate or control activity in society or the economy.

GOOD GOVERNANCE: EMERGENCE OF THE IDEA

The concept of good governance is not new, but it has gained wide popularity in recent times. The term actually existed in the third world, which are today also referred to as developing countries. Good governance ensures goodness in governance and raise in the level of governance. Good governance directly connected to looking after the welfare of the society and is therefore, connected to peoples' satisfaction with the system to some extent.

Despite its popularity the concept entails ambiguity and bewildering variety of meaning and conceptualization. It is equated with a wide range of ideas not always consistent with one another. For some it may mean less government and for some others it may mean more government (Singh andSachdeva 2012: 313).

Since ancient times the issues related to government and state have drawn the attention of many great thinkers like Plato, Aristotle, Thomas Hobbes, Kautilya, John Rawls and others over time and space throughout the history of development. But debate on good governance and new public management gained popularity world over in the recent past. Due to a number of factors it has drawn attention to various aspects of governance. The social, economic, political and administrative factors have brought the issue to the forefront. The world bank, international monetary fund(IMF), organization of economic cooperation and development (OECD), bilateral donoragencies (like ODA, DFID-UK), Multi national corporations (MNCs), and non governmental organizations(NGOs) have brought the approach of good governance to manage public institutions to the minds of the governments. The concern of the world bank is to improve the capacity of borrower governments to efficiently implement the projects and programmes assisted by it for sustainable development.(Noorjahan Bava, ed, 2004: 323)

According to the United Nation charter -Good governance is grounded in the principles of human rights, transparency, honesty and gender equality.

Good governance is the term that symbolizes the paradigm shift of the role of governments. (Holzer Marc & Kim Byong-Joon (ed.) 2002)

MEANING AND DEFINITIONS OF GOOD GOVERNANCE

Kautilya says in his Arthashstra: 'in the happiness of his subject lies the king's happiness, in their welfare his welfare. He shall not consider as good only that which please him but treat as beneficial to him whatever please his subject'. (Singh and Sachdeva, 2012: 313)

Good governance, "among other things participatory, transparent and accountable. It is also an effective and equitable. And it promotes the rule of law" (UNDP).

Good governance "encompasses the role of public authorities in establishing the environment in which economic operators function and in determining the distribution of benefits as well as the relationship between the ruler and the ruled" (OECD).

It is "epitomized by predictable open and enlightened policy making a bureaucracy imbued with a professional ethos; an executive aim of government accountable for its actions' and a strong civil society participating in public affairs and all behaving under the rule of law" (The World Bank 1994 Governance: The World Bank Experience).

Good governance is possible only if three objectives are achieved:

(a) Quality of law and effective implementation of law.

(b) There should be opportunity for every individual to realize his full potential.

(c) There should be effective productivity and no waste in any sector.

In 1998 the concept of governance was for the first time highlighted in a World Bank document on sub- Saharan Africa. By good governance was meant, at that time, sound development. In this context, World Bank identified four key dimensions:

(a) Public sector management.

(b) Accountability

(c) Legal framework for development.

(d) Information and transparency.

In 1992 the World Bank document "Government and Developmen" said that "good governance is central to creating and sustaining an environment which foster strong and equitable development and it is an essential complement to sound economic policies". In this document three distinct aspects are identified in the conceptualization of governance:

(a) the form of political regime (parliamentary or presidential, military or civilian and authoritarian or democratic)

(b) the process by which authority is exercised in the management of the country's economic resources.

(c) The capacity of government to design, formulate and implement policies and in general to discharge government function.

Mechanisms for assuring good governance have three key elements:

(a) internal rules and restrains (for example, internal accounting and auditing systems, independence of judiciary, and the central bank, civil service and budgeting rules);

(b) "voice" and partnership (for example, public private deliberation councils, and service delivery survey to solicit client feedback); and

(c) Competition (for example, competitive social service delivery, private participation in infrastructure, alternative dispute resolution mechanism, outright privatization of certain market driven activities)-WDR 1997.

In other cases, the definition of good governance goes further than mechanisms and purposes that good governance be equated with specific outcomes- in a Rawlsian sense of assuring hat everyone, irrespective of social or economic status, has a voice in governing and receives just fair, equitable treatment. For example, the UNDP notes that , "Good governance is, among other things, participatory, transparent and accountable. It is also effective and equitable. And it promotes the rule of law. Good governance ensures that political, social and economic priorities are based on broad consensus in society and that the voices of poorest and the most vulnerable are heard in decision making over the allocation of development resources".

In general, this initiative will take as a starting point, the five dimensions of good governance that was developed in the World Bank's corruption study for Europe and central Asia and contained in the bank's most recent update of its public sector strategy:

(1) public sector management,

(2) competitive private sector management,

(3) structure of government,

(4) civil society participation and voice, and

(5) political accountability. (Reforming public institutions and strenghthening governance: A World Bank strategy-implementation update", March 28, 2002).

The World Bank also documented the conditionality of good governance. Because economic, human and institutional development are considered important in bringing about sound development management. Governance is a continuum and not necessarily unidirectional; it does not automatically improve over time. It is a plant that needs constant tending. Citizen need to demand good governance. Their ability to do so is enhanced by literacy, education, and employment opportunities. Government need to prove responsive to those demands. Neither of these can be taken for granted. Change occurs sometimes in response to external or internal threats. It also occurs through pressures from different interest group, some of which may be in the form of populist demand. Although lenders and aid agencies and other outsiders can contribute resources and ideas to improve governance, for change to be effective it must be rooted firmly in the societies concerned and can not be imposed from outside". (Word Bank 'Government and Development" Washington DC, 1992).

Most of the literary works on good governance draw from the findings of the World Bank brought out time to time in their reports as a follow up corresponding to their aids to the countries.

According to Andrian Leftwich, in good governance there are three main features-

(1) it promotes open market friendly and competitive economy

(2) promote democratization

(3) Improvement of human rights record.

Minocha defines good governance as "political accountability, availability of freedom, law abiding, bureaucratic accountability, information available transparently, being effective and cooperation between government and society". (Singh and Sachdeva, 2012).

Mohit Bhattacharya says that there are three way of understanding this concept:

(1) It is an attempt to widen the scope of public administration by going beyond formal government.

(2) It is an externally directed term invented to prescribe aid-conditionality

(3) Good governance need not be narrowly conceived in the manner the World Bank and other funding agencies have sought to present them. A more creative approach would be to treat the issues as new opportunities to have a fresh look at state- society relationships in today's complex world of governance.

For the requirement of the good governance The Human Development Report 2002 has identified a few reasons. From the perspective of the human development report, good governance is the same as democratic governance.

INDICATORS OF GOOD GOVERNANCE

World Bank document on Sub-Saharan Africa said that good governance meant sound management. It has identified the following indicators for good governance:

(1) Participation: participation by both men and women is a key cornerstone of good governance. It could be either direct or through legitimate intermediate institutions or representatives. It is important to point out that representative democracy does not necessarily mean that the concerns of the most vulnerable in the society would be taken into consideration in decision making. Participation needs to be informed and organized. This means freedom of association and expression on the one hand and an organized civil society on the other. Rule of law of good governance requires fair legal frameworks that are enforced impartially. It also requires full protection of human rights, particularly those of minorities. Impartial enforcement of laws requires an independent judiciary and an impartial and incorruptible police force.

(2) Transparency: Transparency means that decisions are taken and their enforcement done in a manner that follows rules and regulations. It also means that information is freely available and directly accessible to those who could be effected by such decisions and their enforcement. It also means that enough information is provided and that it is provided in easily understandable forms and media.

(3) Responsiveness: Good governance requires that institutions and processes try to serve all stakeholders within a reasonable timeframe and adhere to the concept of response-ability, that is, responsibility in its letter and spirit.

(4) Consensus-oriented: There are several actors and as many viewpoints in a given society. Good governance requires mediations of different interests in society to reach a broad consensus in society on what is in the best interest of the whole community and how this can be achieved. It also requires a broad and long term perspectives on what is needed for sustainable human development and how to achieve the goals of such development. This can only result from an understanding of the historical, cultural and social contexts of a given society or community.

(5) Equity and inclusiveness: A society's well being depends on ensuring that all its members feel that they have a stake in it and do not feel excluded from the mainstream of the society. This requires involvement of all groups, but particularly the most vulnerable have opportunities to improve or maintain their wellbeing.

(6) Effectiveness and efficiency: Good governance means that process and institutions produce results that meet the needs of the society while making the best use of resources at their disposal. The concept of efficiency in the context of good governance also covers the sustainable use of natural resources and the protection of the environment.

(7) Accountability: Accountability is a key requirement of good governance. Not only governmental institutions but also the private sector and the civil society organizations must be accountable to the public and to their institutional stakeholders. Accountability varies depending on whether decisions or actions taken are internal or external to an organization or institution in general, an organization or an institution is accountable to those who would be affected by its decisions or actions. Accountability can not be enforced without transparency and rule of law. It is claimed as one of the advantages of good governance, but how would this be ensured? Traditionally, in a parliamentary system, political accountability of the executive is to the voters through elected assemblies. Administrative and legal accountability of the executive branch is through administrative procedures and law courts. But if decision making and implementation is now to be shared with private interest, it may become difficult to fix political responsibility.

(8) Contestability: Contestability is about competition to achieve value for money in service delivery. There is greater evidence to suggest that services provided by the publics sector are more expensive than those provided by the private sector. Contestability means choice in the provision of sendees through open competition between potential providers.

Good governance is associated with efficient and effective administration, administration must be citizen friendly, citizen caring and responsive. Good governance requires clarity about responsibilities, access to information about how the government works and using competition to achieve value for money in service delivery.

COMPONENTS OF GOOD GOVERNANCE

The studies reported in the Indian journal of Public Administration (IJPA) 1998 by prominent writers (O.P Minocha, Mohit Bhattacharya, Subash C.Kashyap, Ashok Mukhopadhyay, Bata.K.Dey, R.C. Sekar, Yatish Mishra, 1998 and Madhav Godbole, 1997, Pardeep Sahni, 2003, V. Prasad,

2003 and Haragopal G. 2003), pointed out the following as main components of good governance at all levels (Central, State, Local) of government. These are:

(1) mobilization and utilization of natural resources for betterment of society,

(2) maintenance of macroeconomic stabilization,

(3) providing suitable living environment,

(4) interaction among the government, civil society and private sector,

(5) respect for democratic institutions and human rights and values,

(6) citizen caring and responsive administration,

(7) providing safety and security to the people,

(8) control of corruption and corrupt practices,

(9) emphasis on organizational effectiveness,

(10) capacity building of the communities,

(11) ensuring peoples participation,

(12) satisfying the expectations of all the stakeholders- including customers, employees, suppliers,

(13) compliance of standards set by the investors,

(14) maintenance of honesty and ethics rather than imposition of legislation forcefully in the societal organization,

(15) organizational pluralism-state, market and societal organizations for governance,

(16) transparent administrative system,

(17) competitive government, injecting competition into service delivery,

(18) performance partnership between government, NGOs and private agencies

(19) E-Governance.

All these factors are important for achieving sustainable development in any society. (Satyanarayan, 2004:324)

Along with the good governance World Bank also talked about some main symptoms of poor governance, these symptoms are:

Due to poor governance no clear distinctions are made between private and public. Hence, there is a strong tendency to divert public resources to private gain.

Laws and regulations are not enforced properly, there is often delay in the implementation. Arbitrariness in the application of rules and laws.

Lack of transparency or non transparent decision making.

Privatized production and market led growth do not succeed unless investors face clean rules and institution. (M. Bhattacharya, 2011)

Due to the absence of proper accounting system, budgetary policies can not be monitored or implemented. These systems encourage corruption and distort public investment priorities.

ACCOUNTABILITY AND GOOD GOVERNANCE

The accountability is an essential prerequisite of "good governance". (World Bank 1992). Good governance is itself an accountability-oriented concept applicable to a specific target group mainly Third World countries. Governments are the main producers of public goods, and they frame rules for the market to work efficiently. The institutional frameworks conducive to growth and poverty alleviation do not evolve on their own; rather the emergence of such frameworks need incentive and adequate institutional capacity to create and sustain them. (Bhattacharya, 2011)

The World Bank pinpointed accountability as an essential prerequisite of "good governance" (World Bank 1992). Banks accountability concern in the context of structural adjustment policy, has pervaded both public and private sectors. The phenomenon of "capture" of public services and resources by relatively narrow special interest has been a common feature in most countries. Accountability assumes importance in respect of ensuring efficiency in investment as well as in production and distribution of public goods and services. Government has also to ensure accountability in the private sector through appropriate company and security legislation, competitive policy regulatory oversight, especially when "down sizing of government". (Bhattacharya, 2011) takes place through disinvestments, privatization and contracting.

According to the World Bank document public accountability involves three interrelated groups:

(a) The general public and particularly recipients of public services, who are interested in service providers being accountable to them.

(b) Political leaders and supervisors of service providers who would like the service providers to be accountable to them.

(d) The service providers themselves whose objectives and interest often differ from those of (a) and (b).

Historically accountability revealed three features:

(1) the silence of micro-level accountability, as due to expansion of state activity it has become difficult to apply broad accountability to numerous functions of government;

(2) the focus in accountability tends to be on inputs, especially public expenditure, rather than outputs or effect;

(3) accountability has mostly been by internal administrative control exercised by political leader, government agencies and bureaucrats acting as proxies for the public. (M. Bhattacharya, 2011).

World Bank identified two broad types of accountability: micro accountability and macro accountability. Micro accountability remain critical, especially in ensuring government responsiveness to the views and the need of the publics for which services are intended. The concepts of "exit" and "voice" which originated in Albert O. Hirschman's classic work, Exit,Voice and Loyalty: Responses to Decline in Firms, Organizations, and State (1970) have been used to underscore the importance of micro accountability. For instance, competition or scope for the public to 'exit' when dissatisfied with a service, may have a salutary effect on the agency concerned by reducing its revenues and then by making the careers or pay of the staff less secure. Similarly, 'voice', in the sense of participation of the public may influence the quality or volume of a service through some form of articulation of preferences of demand. Accountability is increased if such 'voice' makes the public agency more responsive to public demands.

Accountability at the micro level can, however, be sustain only when the government and society at large are committed for doing so.

The other kind of accountability is macro-accountability. The macro-accountabilityhas two major dimensions:

(1) Financial accountability,

(2) Accountability for overall economic performance.

As the World Bank document, financial accountability involves:

(1) A properly functioning government accounting system for effective expenditure control and cash management;

(2) An external audit system which reinforces expenditure control by exposure and sanctions against misspending and corruption;

(3) Mechanisms to review and act on the results of audits and to ensure that follow up action is taken to remedy problems identified.

Accountability for overall economic performance involves review of resource use in public investment programs and general strengthening of the capacity of governments to monitor and evaluate their own economic performance including proper resources use.

Accountability is about power-about people having not just a say in official decisions but also the right to hold their rulers to account. They can demand answers to questions about decisions and actions. And they can sanction public officials or bodies that do not live up to their responsibilities. Today the insistence that public officials be held accountable is extending to corporations, multinational organizations and others who have more power in public decision-making. Because of the their influence over the lives of people and communities, they are holders of the public trust and so answerable for their actions to national legislatures and to the public. Accountability means different things in different contexts. To whom, for what and by which standards is accountability judged? Often the concern is with sanctions against legal wrongdoing.

All these kinds of accountability are central to democratic governance to ensuring that the holders of the public trust are acting effectively and fairly. (*UNDP*, Human Development Report, 2002: 65)

DEMOCRATIC GOVERNANCE VS GOOD GOVERNANCE

Democratic governance differs from the concept of 'good governance' in recognizing that political and civil freedoms and participation have basic value as developmental ends in themselves and not just means for achieving socio-economic progress.

Democratic governance is built on the concept of human development in its full sense of the term, which is about expanding capabilities people have, to be free and able to lead lives that they would choose to. The capability to be free from threats of violence, and to be able to speak freely is as important as being literate for a full life. While the range of capabilities that people have is huge and almost infinite, several key capabilities are fundamental in human life and are universally valued, not only those in the 'socioeconomic sphere' such as health and survival, education and access to knowledge, minimum material means for a decent standard of living, but those in the 'political sphere' such as security from violence, and political freedom and participation. Indeed, these are core elements of human well being reflected in the Millennium Declaration.

Democratic governance needs to be underpinned by a political regime that guarantees civil and political liberties as human rights, and that ensures participation of people and accountability of decision makers. (UNDP Human development Report, 2002)

Democratic governance implies to the very functioning of the system in a democratic manner. Within the mechanism of running the state there is participation and accountability. the state organs perform in a democratic manner. Each organ of the government has certain autonomy and freedom to act upon and take decisions, and at the same time also accountable for decisions taken.

Good governance need not necessarily have democratic governance. The distinction between the two is that in good governance the focus is on equal distribution of development and efficient policy implementation, in democratic governance it is more to do with method adopted for governance.

Democratic governance is meaningful as it is a means to achieve good governance. In a democratic country to achieve good governance is not always easy.

***Democratic Governance means*:**

- People's human rights and fundamental freedoms are respected, allowing them to live with dignity.
- People have a say in decisions that affect their lives.
- People can hold decision-makers accountable.
- Inclusive and fair rules, institutions and practices govern social interactions.
- Women are equal partners with men in private and public spheres of life and decision making.
- People are free from discrimination based on race, ethnicity, class, gender or any other attribute.
- The needs of future generations are reflected in current policies.
- Economic and social policies are responsive to people's needs and aspirations.

In democratic governance there is a provision for people's participation in decision making e.g. as in the case of Indian Panchayati Raj for rural administration and municipal corporation for urban administration.

Success of good governance depends on democratic governance. Only in the democratic atmosphere through democratic means that good governance can be achieved, it is the responsibility of all democratically elected governments to ensure that state institutions follow democratic means as laid down in the constitution. Good governance has been defined sometimes in terms of goals, sometimes in terms of means, sometimes left entirely to democratic choice of goals, and sometimes with pre-ordained goals.

According to Human Development Report 2002, democratic governance means –

(a) people's human rights and fundamental r freedoms are respected, allowing them to live in dignity;

(b) people can hold decisions, which are accountable;

(c) Private and public spheres of life and decision making. The needs of future generations are reflected in current policies.

(d) Economic and social policies aim at eradicating poverty and expending the choice that all people have in their lives.

More countries than ever before are working to build democratic governance. Their challenge is to develop institutions and processes that are more responsive to the needs of ordinary citizens, including the poor, and that promote development. UNDP helps countries strengthen electoral and legislative systems, improve access to justice and public administration and develop a greater capacity to deliver basic services to those most in need.

In 2001, the United Nations Development Programme (UNDP) established the Democratic Governance Thematic Trust Fund (DGTTF) which is the primary mechanism through which donor partners channel non-core contributions to UNDP's activities on democratic governance. The main function of this funding mechanism is to provide country offices with discretionary funds to explore innovative approaches in democratic governance in politically sensitive environments and within the areas of inclusive participation, responsive institutions or international principles. (UNDP)

The greatest threats to good governance come from corruption, violence and poverty, all of which undermine transparency, security, participation and fundamental freedoms. Democratic governance advances development, by bringing its energies to bear on such tasks as eradicating poverty, protecting the environment, ensuring gender equality, and providing for sustainable livelihoods. It ensures that civil society plays an active role in setting priorities and making the needs of the most vulnerable people in society known.

Well-governed countries are less likely to be violent and less likely to be poor. When the alienated are allowed to speak and their human rights are protected, they are less likely to turn to violence as a solution. When the poor are given a voice, their governments are more likely to invest in national policies that reduce poverty. In so doing, good governance provides the setting for the equitable distribution of benefits from growth.

"...as we all know, infrastructure is not just a matter of roads, schools and power grids. It is equally a question of strengthening democratic governance and the rule of law. Without accountability, not only of the government to its people but of the people to each other, there is no hope for a viable democratic State." (Secretary-General Ban Ki-moon, 19 February 2009)

The link between both greater and lower quality of governance:

i) First of all, democracies allow populations to peacefully and regularly oust inept, inefficient and corrupt government administrations, while allowing people to keep more efficient, successful regimes, thus tending to make the quality of governance on average higher in the long run.

On the other hand, authoritarian regimes may randomly provide high-quality governance, but if they do not, they can only be changed by force, which may take years or decades longer than under democratic institutions.

As Sen summarizes in considering the effects of democracy relative to authoritarian regimes:

"We have to consider the political incentives that operate on governments and on the persons and groups that are in office. The rulers have the incentive to listen to what people want if they have to face their criticism and seek their support in elections." (Amartya Sen 2002).

According to the USAID's report on "Foreign Aid in the National Interest", the two are mutually reinforcing: when they develop together, resources are used to advance the public good.

- Public institutions perform their designated roles.
- Social consensus supports and stabilizes the system of government.
- Disputes are settled peacefully.
- And investment flows into the country, attracted by the low transaction costs associated with government transparency and legitimacy and the rule of law. (also because of low risk under stable governments)

ECONOMIC DEVELOPMENT AND GOVERNANCE

According to the *Human Development Report 1996*, published by the United Nations Development Program, "human development is the end—economic growth a means."

It is true that economic growth, by increasing a nation's total wealth, also enhances its potential for reducing poverty and solving other social problems.

But history offers a number of examples where economic growth was not followed by similar progress in human development. Instead growth was achieved at the cost of greater inequality, higher unemployment, weakened democracy, loss of cultural identity, or over consumption of natural resources needed by future generations.

According to the classical definition given by the United Nations World Commission on Environment and Development in 1987, development is sustainable if it "meets the needs of the present without compromising the ability of future generations to meet their own needs."

Development is measured by the extent to which the skewed distribution of property ownership is corrected; by the number of people brought above the poverty line; by the spread of education, health, and housing services; by employment generation, economic growth and price stability; by political participation of the unorganized and disinherited majority; and by cultural progress. Usually economic development is so over emphasized that development becomes synonymous with economic development. Even social development is related economic development and even the spiritual aspect of human life is not related to economic development. (Singh and Sachdeva 2012: 331)

United Nations defines development as:

(a) accelerated economic growth, more equitable distribution of wealth and income,

(b) Full utilization of manpower and better utilization of national resources. It has a social context.

(c) Social services being made available to the needy sections of the people.

(d) Social welfare services being made available to women, children and handicapped, etc.

(e) Protection of human environment.

According to World Bank document economic development ideally refers to the sustained, concerted actions of communities and policymakers that improve the standard of living and economic health of a specific locality. The definition of economic development given by Professor Michael Todaro is an improvement in living conditions, improvement of the citizens self-esteem needs and free and a just society. He suggests that the most accurate method of measuring economic development is the Human Development Index which takes into account the literacy rates and life expectancy which in-turn has an outright impact on productivity and could lead to Economic growth. However, economic development can also be measured by taking into account the GDI (gender related index).

Economic development will only be successful if the whole nation is willing to give their best efforts towards its achievement. A lot of theories have been forwarded by different schools of thought about how economic development should be achieved. Many economists have suggested that each country should try to achieve modernization and industrialization in order to achieve economic development. Economic development leads to improvements in many sectors of a nation. Economic development has to be supported by the whole nation from economists, politicians, and also civilians.

Economic development is directly connected to the governance. It depends on the policy taken by the government for the economic growth.

The issue of sustainable development is concerned with enhancing human well being through time. What constitutes good life is highly subjective, and the relative importance accorded to different aspects of wellbeing varies with individuals, societies and generations. (Satyanarayan 2004)

United Nation Development Program (UNDP) has observed that eliminating poverty, creating jobs and sustaining livelihood, protecting and regenerating the environment and promoting advancement of women are the most critical elements of sustainable development in the 21st century.

GOOD GOVERNANCE FOR HUMAN RIGHTS

According to the UN High Commissioner for Human Rights, the true test of "good" governance is the degree to which it delivers on the promise of human rights: civil, cultural, economic, political and social rights. The key question is: are the institutions of governance effectively guaranteeing the right to health, adequate housing, sufficient food, quality education, fair justice and personal security?

The concept of good governance has been clarified by the work of the Commission on Human Rights. Its resolution 2000/64 expressly linked good governance to an enabling environment conducive to the enjoyment of human rights and "prompting growth and sustainable human development."

By linking good governance to sustainable human development, emphasizing principles such as accountability, participation and the enjoyment of human rights, the resolution stands as an implicit endorsement of the rights-based approach to development.

In its resolution 2001/72, the Commission on Human Rights reaffirmed its earlier resolution by consensus.

The following section builds on the ideas of democracy and democratic governance, that is, good governance relative to the development process. (UNHCHR 2001)

GOOD GOVERNANCE: INDIAN SCENARIO

When we talk about good governance in the Indian context, one can not help but look at the examples found in the political history of the country. Indian historiography is full of such examples. During the early stage of state formations in ancient time, the concept of 'Janapadas' emerged in which people and territory are combined. The king or 'rajan' who until now was ruling only over his people identified territories on which his people lived. There are also instances of 'ganas' which are more republic type in the nature of administration with no monarch but few ruling elites who looked after the needs and security of the people.

The treatise of Kautilya is well referred to by scholars working on the importance of good governance. The philosophy of good governance was embedded in the understanding of right from wrong, being able to differentiate good from bad, just from unjust and moral from immoral. In Arthashastra the emphasis is on the conduct of the king as the head of the state, whose responsibility was well-being of the subjects. A good ruler is one who is far sighted and is prepared for the most extraordinary situations. It also emphasizes on the personal conduct of the ruler. During the Maurya period, even Ashoka placed great importance on the personal conduct of the king. There are ample evidences to show that king Ashoka set an example of good governance by following the principles of Buddhism. The administrative machinery that was set up during his regime was with the single objective of achieving good governance. The manner in which the elaborate bureaucracy functioned draws attention to the methods adopted by one of the most well known rulers of ancient India. During the Mughal period it was Akbar who again set examples of good governance. All of these great rulers tried to project themselves as the benevolent father figure, who is always prepared to take care of the subjects and their needs, but at the same time authoritative enough to maintain the rule of law.

In the modern context when we are talking about good governance, one question that comes to mind is: whether it is possible to apply the political ideology that dictated the governance of historical time. The idea of governance in modern India is influenced by the western notion of nation-state. The framers of our constitution took into account the needs of a country that is so hugely diverse culturally and socially. The provisions embodied in the constitution are meant to safeguard the interest of the citizens. The objective of the constitution is to secure justice for all irrespective of caste, creed, gender and religious differences. In order to carry out the job of ruling the country India inherited a structured bureaucratic system from the British that included armed forces for the national security. As a democratic country India has all the paraphernalia required for the kind of development and progress a nation aspires for. However, mere presence of the provisions in the constitution to safeguard and promote the interest of the citizens as a whole does not guarantee the same if it is not accompanied by good governance. It is also dependent on strong political will to make sure that the constitutional provisions are utilized to the best capacity and it is where India seemed to have lagged behind. Some of the ongoing political and social crises that the country is facing comes from the fact that state organs have failed to execute welfare measures in the right spirit. Though efforts have been made towards achieving good governance at various levels including making the system more transparent by bringing in acts like RTI (Right to Information), PIL (Public Interest Litigation), involving civil society and NGOs and the most recent being the introduction of Lokayuktas to address discrepancies in the government administration, it still will take long for India to achieve the kind of development that is associated with a welfare state.

Keeping in mind the diversity of the state independent India has constituted laws for the protection of the rights of social, cultural and religious minority groups. For the social and economic upliftment of the backward communities special provisions have been made. The reservation system of Indian government aims to bridge the social and economic disparity that exist in the country.

CHALLENGES TO GOOD GOVERNANCE

One common problem that most of the developing countries face today is related to good governance. The failure to provide a clean administration by the governments make way for break down of the system. The very nature of politics of a particular country also can pose a challenge to the governance. In a country like India where multiparty system has become the norm and is seen as the true representative of democratic principles, it has its own disadvantages as well. It is also acknowledged largely that for the success of any system and sustained development, political stability is a prerequisite. In a multiparty system the challenge is to have stability, as seen in the case of India today.

Some of the major challenges to good governance are:

Bureaucracy

One of the major problems in bureaucracy is to do with accountability and red tapism. Many of the good policies introduced by the government fail to reach the beneficiaries due to bureaucratic hurdles. There is lack of commitment and many a times due to the unresponsive attitude of the bureaucrats service delivery is compromised or delayed. Reform in bureaucracy therefore becomes necessary in the context of good governance. In the present context bureaucrats function as providers and regulator but not as facilitators. Unless the bureaucrats are made accountable in the functioning of the system good governance seem like a distant dream. An efficient Bureaucracy can transform the face of a country through speedy policy implementation and service distribution. The presence of redtapism in bureaucracy provide space for corruption and this one area where most countries face problems. Thus bureaucracy is one of the biggest challenges to good governance.

Judiciary

Judiciary is independent of political, executive and legislative controls, it is an independent body, and have all the power to give judgments fearlessly. But most of the time judiciary delay in giving the judgment. In a democratic system justice delayed is justice denied. Judiciary system must be simplified in order to make it easily accessible to all sections of the society. Upholding the spirit of justice and the preamble of the constitution that all are equal in the eyes of law is important for the citizen to have trust in the system. Disposition of justice is closely related to good governance.

Federal system

Another important challenge to good governance is federal system. In federal system the power is divided between centre and the state. Though it has its own advantages it also has certain disadvantages. A federal polity is more than the provisions made in the constitution; its actual shape is determined by its actual working in practice. In a country like India where there is wide regional variations conflicts may occur between centre and the state. Smooth or timely implementation of policy depends on the centre state relationship. In the context of good governance it is again the role of the bureaucracy that become crucial. In the absence of national monitoring system states often tend to shrug responsibility and accountability in policy implementation.

Institutional structures

In any form of government institutional roles can not be underplayed for the success and failure of governance. The internal structures of various institutions that are part of administrative machinery may also pose a challenge to a good governance. Government and non government institutions facilitate for developmental projects, generating avenue for employment, maintaining law and order etc. Democratization of institutional structure becomes important in order to achieve good governance.

Social security

Social security continue to be the most critical area in the context of good governance. Facilitating for social development like primary education and health care, improved condition of living, drinking water, pension schemes, subsidized food to the poor through PDS (public distribution system) and ensuring justice available though local courts. These are some of the responsibilities state cannot overlook not withstanding investment in capitalist sectors and emphasis on liberalization, privatization and outsourcing services that has become the practice of a globalized economy.

Corruption

Biggest hurdle to good governance is corruption. There is no country in the world which is corruption free. It is found in all society in varying degrees and nature. While in developed countries corruption take place at the highest level that may involve important government figures, in developing countries it is much more wide spread and may be experienced at all levels. It is not limited to government institution alone and are found even in private institution. Deep rooted corruption in politics and governance can threaten the very foundation of any system. Instances of corruption even in judiciary are noticed across the world.

Economy

In the economic front good governance completely depends on the policy making and strategy based on general consensus. Developmental projects for economic growth must be equally distributed across the country and mindless extraction of natural resources leads to large scale exploitation of it. One of the biggest challenges in economic development is to do with equity. There must be careful reconsideration of subsidies in agriculture and public sectors like power, energy, oil, transport, telecommunication and other such areas.

Political

Another most important challenges to good governance is the need for political reforms. Instability of the government not only at the centre but in the state as well creating lots of hurdle for the development. Many third world countries adopted British model parliamentary system but the essential conditions for its success requires-a well organized, ideologically oriented and fairly stable system of two major political parties- which does not exist in most of these countries. Political reforms cannot be complete without electoral reforms which would ensure good candidates being elected; election commission authorized to disqualify a person found guilty for corrupt practices; provision of compulsory maintenance of accounts by political parties and audit thereof by agencies specified by the election commission; regulation of donations given by the companies to the political parties; strengthening the existing provision regarding registration and de-registration of political parties; curbing the role of money power in the election and rationalization of the size of electorate for each constituency.

The term 'good governance' has continuously evolved with the development of human civilization. Good governance is a notion broader than that of good government and the success of a government is dependent on meaningful development. Most international organizations for human development cite the examples of poor policy planning and execution in development practices. Despite having achieved sound technological advancement many well meant projects and programmes fail to deliver the desired results. Market oriented private investors face the difficulty of clearing the rules and regulations of institutions. At the same time, failure to involve larger beneficiaries like civil society, create distrust towards the investors that often end up in confrontation and litigation.

While the citizens can and should demand for good governance, it is the responsibility of any government to keep welfare of the people at the core of the policy making. Contemporary view on public organization is that of imperfectionist one, however, there is no one single model of government that can be called 'utopian'. Though democracy is hailed as the best model of administration with provisions for incorporating public opinion in policy making through civil society, proper and efficient execution of policy remain a problem. It is the people in organizations of the larger state structure who play important role in public administration. Centralized structure is seen as a hurdle by those who advocate the modern concept of public administration through decentralization of power that allow lower level functioning units to interpret rules and regulations to suit the local needs and to innovate new methods under changed situations. An example of this maybe drawn from the local village level administration where the villagers in the Panchayat decides to utilize resources according to their needs. Good governance can become a reality when stake holders partake in the process of planning and execution, and in a democratic system such a reality is possible with good political intention.

REFERENCES

1. Bidyut Chakrabarty and Prakash Chand, 2012. *Public Administration in a Globalizing World: Theories and Practices*, Sage Publication, New Delhi, pp.122-130.
2 Mohit Bhattacharya, 2011. *New Horizon of Public Administration*, Jawahar Publishers and Distributors, New Delhi, pp. 408-426.
3. Hoshiar Singh and Pardeep Sachdeva, 2012. *Public Administration Theory and Practice*, Pearson, Noida

4. The World Bank, 1992. Governance and Development, D.C.
5. Jan Kooiman(ed), 1993. *Modern Governance: New Government-Society Interactions,* New Delhi, Sage Publication.
6. O.P. Minocha, 1998. "Good Governance: New Public Management Perspective", *Indian Journal of Public Administration,* July-September.
7. Riviera-Batiz Francisco L., "Democracy, Governance and Economic Growth: Theory & Evidence". *Paper presented at conference on Democracy, Participation and Development held in 1999 New York.*
8. Noorjahan Bava,(ed), 2004. *Public Administration in the 21st Century,* Kanishka Publishers & Distributors, New Delhi, pp. 322-326.
9. UNDP, *Human Development Report, 2002.*
10. World Bank, *World Bank Development Report, 1992-1998*
11. www. oecd.org/dac/
12. UNDP Report, 1997. Government for Sustainable Human Development.

2

CITIZENS, THEIR RIGHTS AND OBLIGATIONS

MANILA NARZARY*

According to Jean Bodin, a 16th century jurist, 'a citizen is one who enjoys the common liberty and protection of authority or state'. Citizen is a person who owes allegiance to a state and in turn receives protection from the state. According to Aristotle citizen is 'he who has the power to take part in the deliberative or judicial administration of any state, and generally speaking, a state is a body of citizens sufficing for the purpose of life'. (Anupama Roy: 2008: 132) Citizens have certain rights and duties, which vary from one country to another. Citizen must fulfill his duties and obligations towards the state.

Citizen may be defined as those who are and who are not member of the common society. The social and political ties which hold an individual in community with his fellows is the essence of the citizenship. A citizen need to understand that his roles includes status, a sense of loyalty, the discharge of certain duties and the enjoyment of rights not at individual level but in the relation to the state as well. In modern times, citizens have a right to participate in politics but also have a right to pursue their private commitments, besides their political commitment. But understanding citizens' rights and obligations is not possible without understanding 'citizenship' which is a political term used to explain a person's relationship with the state.

---

* Assistant Professor, Deptt. of Political Science, Kalindi College, Univ. of Delhi

What is Citizenship?

Many thinkers have defined citizenship in various ways. According to T. H. Marshall, "citizenship is essentially a matter of ensuring that everyone is treated as a full and equal member of society and the way to ensure this sense of membership is through according people an increasing number of citizenship rights".[1]

Citizenship is, as Laski observes, "The contribution of one's instructed judgement to the public good."

The concept of citizenship has been invented and defined time and again depending upon the changing socio-economic and political realities. Some of the important theories of citizenship in its long history of development are as follows:

The word citizenship is derived from the Latin word civis and its Greek word polites which means member of the polis or city. Citizenship denotes the status of an individual as a full and responsible member of a political community.[2] In political theory citizenship refers not only to a legal status as a member of a particular country but also a normative ideal- the ruled are full and equal participants in the political process. Citizenship is a distinctively political ideal, for people as in a monarchy or a dictatorship are subjects and not citizens.[3] Being part of a political community has been persistent social need as old as settled human community. Besides having rights and duties citizenship is also an identity and is shared in common by different groups in society and thus is integrative in nature. Citizenship also signifies besides membership, the participation of citizen in collective affairs of their government.

In ancient times, this privilege was given only to the selected few. But in the modern times with the spread of democracy this privilege has been given to all the people living in the state. Democratic notion of citizenship differ from the pre-modern conceptions that determined people's status by their ethnicity, gender, religion or class. Citizens are classified as natural and neutralized citizens. The former, are citizen by virtue of birth in particular place, while the latter acquire citizenship. The crucial equalitarian impulse of modern citizenship is based on the principle of one person, one vote.[4] Citizenship is the product of a community where the right to rule is decided by a prescribed procedure which expresses the will of the general body of its members. While asserting their will, nobody is discriminated on grounds of race , religion, gender, place of birth, etc. T.H.Marshall in his *Citizenship and Social Class* (1950) observed that citizenship implies full membership of a community: those who possess this status are equal with respect to the rights and duties associated with it. Marshall adds that different societies will attach different rights and duties to the status of citizen, for there is no universal principle which determines necessary rights and duties of citizenship in general. The original concept of citizenship exclusively focused on the sense of duty where the question of rights was relegated to the background. But in the contemporary society citizenship is primarily concerned with certain rights. In these scheme duties of the individual are accepted only as long as they are considered to be essential for the maintenance of those rights.

The term citizenship is very common throughout the world and it is a central concept of everyday political discourse. Formally it is a relationship between an individual and the state by which the former owes allegiance and the letter owes protection. This relationship is determined and recognized by international law.

With the development of capitalist market relations and the growing influence of liberalism in the nineteenth century, the notion of citizens as individuals with private and conflicting interests gradually gained primacy, as citizenship as civic activity, public spiritedness and active political participation was relegated to a vestigial past. Till most of the twentieth century, the bias in the liberal theory of citizenship in favour of the individual citizen continued and citizenship was seen as a legal status which gave the citizen certain rights assuring protection from state interference.[5]

CLASSICAL THEORIES OF CITIZENSHIP

Greek theory of Citizenship

The idea of citizenship was first developed in ancient Greek and Roman Republics. The concept of citizenship was developed by Aristotle in his book *politics.* In ancient Athens, citizenship was primarily perceived in terms of participation duties. Ancient Greek citizenship was completely different from the present day citizenship. In ancient Greek city state very few inhabitants enjoyed the status of 'freeman' who were treated as full citizens. These citizens were equal among themselves as regards their rights. There was no discrimination between the rich and the poor among freeman. The rest of the community comprised of slaves, women and aliens who had no rights of citizenship. That is why Aristotle regarded citizenship as a privilege of the ruling class. In ancient Greek political tradition this privilege of the ruling class was also regarded to be a part of their duty. All citizens were expected to perform this duty in order to secure good life for themselves as well as for the non citizens. For Aristotle, citizens are men who enjoy the right of the sharing the deliberative or judicial administration of any state and generally speaking a state is a body of citizen s sufficing for the purpose of life. The purpose of the citizen is the salvation of the community. The community is the constitution and the virtue of a citizen is relative to the constitution of which he is a member. Citizenship meant not merely participation in the election of the legislator or the executive authorities but direct or active share in the exercise of deliberate and judicial functions in which the sovereign power resided. Citizenship meant the participation in the exercise of sovereignty.

According to Aristotle, participation, deliberative and judicial functions of the state demands a high degree of moral and intellectual excellence, which he terms as 'virtue' and this virtue is not to be found in all inhabitants of the state. The slaves and women are not considered citizens because they do not have deliberative faculty. The aliens can not be citizens because they are inhabitant of other city-state. He stipulated that the young and old could not be a citizen for former was immature and the latter infirm. Aristotle pointed out that in order to discharge the functions effectively citizen needed to inhabit a polis that was compact and close-knit.

Aristotle says that the citizen should know both how to rule and how to obey. Citizens are all who share in the civic life of ruling and being ruled in turn. They must possess the knowledge and the capacity requisite for ruling as well as being ruled. Aristotle believed in the dictum that he who has never learnt to obey can not be a good commander. He also considered a good citizen is someone who could live in harmony with the constitution and enough experience, education and leisure time to devote himself to task and responsibilities of active citizenship. A good citizen would possess virtue or moral goodness that would help in realizing a selfless and cooperative civic life.

Roman Theory of Citizenship

Rome developed a pragmatic, flexible and legalistic notion of citizenship. Romans developed a form of citizenship which was more complex, flexible and legalistic. The basic difference from the Greek was that it was extended to the plebeians, underprivileged aliens domiciled in Rome, traders and merchants. In Rome citizens entailed six privileges:

(a) service in the army;

(b) voting to the assembly;

(c) eligibility to public office;

(d) legal right to action and appeal;

(e) intermarriage; and

(f) trade with other Roman citizens.

In the fourth century, Rome's basic concept of citizenship underwent three historically significant adaptations. In 381 BC Rome conferred full citizenship on the male members of the city of Tusculum in the region of Latium. The distinction between 'Latin' and 'Roman' citizenship was also introduced so that a person could simultaneously be a citizen of his own city and of Rome. Five decades later the inhabitants of the other Latin towns were offered partial citizenship that allowed enjoyment of private privileges. Roman citizenship was conferred to the inhabitants of the territories that Rome annexed, quite contrary to the practice of the Greek, who continued to treat the citizens of neighbouring Greek cities as aliens. Roman citizenship provided total equality before the law. As with Greek citizenship, in Roman citizenship virtue meant the willingness to serve one's state. Service to the state meant military rather than juridical political service.[6] Only the people of lowest rank like women were excluded from the benefit of citizenship. However, different categories of citizens were entitled to different types of rights, a practice which is not applicable to the modern concept of citizenship.

Republicanism Theory of Citizenship:

During the medieval Europe political authority was eclipsed by ecclesiastical authority. Temporal citizenship was no longer considered to be important in the fifteen and the sixteen century with the advent of modern thought, the idea of citizenship again occupied the centre stage in Italian republics. Niccolo Machiavelli, the famous Italian thinker gave a new lease of life to this idea. Machiavelli, for whom the virtue of the citizens is the greatest input to Rome's greatness, revives the classical arguments of citizenship in the Roman, rather than the Aristotelian sense. Reflecting on the instability and vulnerability of his native city Florence and comparing it with the power and stability that Rome achieved. Machiavelli says that the key factor is citizen virtue, which means patriotism, self-discipline, simple piety and the willingness to subordinate private gain for public goods. Machiavelli also emphasized on the need for a citizen army as the quintessence of citizenship, for a citizen, as opposed to a mercenary soldier, is reliable enough to scarifies his life for the unity of his state.[7]

Similarly, the French philosopher Bodin in his book *Six Books of the Commonwealth* (1962, translated version) devoted two chapters on citizenship. He rejected definitions which emphasized eligibility for public office or enjoyment of rights and privileges. Bodin's concern is with the legal and social dimensions of citizenship, for he states that birth, adoption or enfranchisement can be the basis for acquiring citizenship. What was modern in Bodin's theory of citizenship was that he subjected the whole body of citizens to single sovereign power, inspite of diversity of laws, language, customs, religion or race. He rejects the idea of equal citizenship for all as no state ever recognizes its citizens to be equal in rights and privileges. Hobbes and Lock ignore the ideals of classical republicanism and citizen virtue. Lock underlines the importance of individual rights as the basis of legitimate political authority.

CONTEMPORARY THEORIES OF CITIZENSHIP

Liberal Theory of Citizenship

Liberalism gave more importance to the citizen's ability to engage in public discussion believing the good policy emerges out of filtering of such articulation. According to the liberal theory civil rights constitute the foundation of citizenship, liberal theory believe the evolution of the rights associated with the citizenship. T.H. Marshall is regarded as the chief exponent of this theory. Marshall (1950) observed that citizenship prescribes equal rights and duties, liberty and constraints, power and responsibilities for different individuals. Under citizenship the individual come together to decide the terms of their association. According to the liberal theory a social class promotes inequality between different individuals on the basis of ownership of property, level of education and structure of economy, but citizenship tends to bestow equal status upon them. According to Marshall the idea of citizenship begins with the provision of civil rights, and proceeds further by giving rise to political and social rights respectively. It is the responsibility of the state to provide health care, education, and housing to their citizens if they fail to have it. When country is fully developed, the individual no longer remains dependent on the market system. According to liberal theory citizenship assures a share to all individuals in the common heritage of the community, it develops the sense of integration among the people of the community. Besides all these, liberalism also emphasize universality, meaning equal rights for all before the law.

Bentham and Mill, well known utilitarians, says that individual liberty, participation and just appointment of property are the essence of citizenship. Democratic franchise creates space for 'greatest happiness of the greatest number' as the basic principle of citizenship. Democratically elected representatives would pursue policies beneficial to the whole community. One can also find socialist influence in Mill's view that a more just distribution of property and workers participation in the factory were essential for citizenship, for which he cites two reasons: i) those who are industrious and hard working should not only get economic benefits but also political rights, ii) if citizenship is a pact of participation, then this sense of participation should also be reflected in the industry.[8]

Similar view was held by T. H. Green that the essence of citizenship lies in 'promoting the good life for all irrespective of social class; to foster the moral nature of man and to provide a basic minimum of social welfare. A good environment needs to be provided by the state for the citizens to grow and foster self, an important responsibility of the state towards its citizens.

This concept of citizenship has three particular features:

(i) positive freedom i.e., the positive capacity of the individual to develop his personality in the social context,

(ii) abolition of poverty by the state. No one could be worthy citizen if his creative energies are devoted to subsistence,

(iii) the state must ensure a minimum level of welfare for all citizens but at the same time not intervene so forcefully as to weaken the capitalist and property system nor to lessen the individual's self-reliant pursuit of his freedom.[9]

The liberalism theory equated citizenship with an egalitarian state. The political participation which was restricted to the property owning males during nineteenth century, was extended to all including women. Universal adult franchise has become a norm in all democratic countries. The economic and social concept of citizenship was accepted by a number of states such as England, America, and other European countries, although the process has been extremely hesitant.

Libertarian Theory of Citizenship

The chief exponents of this theory is Robert Nozick and F.A.Hayek. According to this theory citizenship is a product of free choice and contract among individuals. Nozick in Anarchy, state, and Utopia (as cited in the Political Theory and Thought by Gauba 2008) observed that individual resorts to private activity, market exchange and voluntary association in order to realize their values, belief and preferences. Both Hayek and Nozick stressed the need to protect the individual's negative freedom against the power of the state. Hayek says that , socialism was the road to serfdom. Their argument is that the objective of the social citizenship of shaping a more equal society is a forlorn hope because people are inherently unequal. This fact of human nature should be accepted and the state should not try to temper with it. The libertarian theory define citizenship in terms of forbearance which means not interfering in the rights of others, rather than actual participation in the realization of certain communal values through political activity and political institutions. The duty of the citizen is not attempt for certain common good but to maintain the legal framework, which secure space for them to realize their private non-civic interest.

Many critics have criticized the libertarian theory in terms of morality of their premise and its practical benefits. According to critics this model of citizenship would lead to sharp disputes and intense clash of interests within society. It has exacerbated the polarization of social classes, the selfish rich at the top and the despairing poor at the bottom.

Communitarian Citizenship

The communitarian theory of citizenship is popularized by number of thinkers like Hannah Arendt, Michal Walzer, Benzamin Barber, Charles Tylor and others. According to this theory a citizen should identify himself with the community of which he is a member, and take active part in its political life . This takes into account the cultural and social context in the discussion of the theory, giving more emphasize to the dimension of national belonging. According to the communitarian theory, the loyalty lies with the community that is a part of the nation and therefore the inherent cultural tradition, social understanding and social customs, belief and practices need to be respected and protected. A person can not contribute substantially to the realization of the common interest if he does not identify himself with the community of which he is a member. Community can be sustained by a notion of common good. Communitarians believe that the individual choices require a secure cultural context and a cultural context requires secure political context. Communitarians tend to favour policies designed to protect and promote ties to the family and family like groups.

But this model of citizenship is only suitable to a small homogeneous society with common traditions and culture which existed at Athens in the fourth century B.C. and Florence in fifteenth century.

Marxist Theory of Citizenship

According to Marxist theory, the idea of equal citizenship rights can not exist in class divided society, for it is always the interests, privileges, rights and powers of the dominant class that is protected. Marxism has been suspicious of citizenship and considered it as being contrary to class interest of proletariat. Marx called the modern democratic citizenship as bourgeois citizenship. According to Marx, political emancipation through citizenship becomes meaningful with human emancipation. Marx mainly talked about the classless society, with collective ownership of means of production and with the end of oppression, citizenship can transcend, class distinctions and class division. Marx did not reject the achievements of modern liberal democratic citizenship and a big step forward within the prevailing scheme of things, he only pointed out that mere political emancipation is not adequate. Socialist society embodies the idea of proletarian internationalism; there is no question of considering citizenship which refers in particular, to the nation state. Marx had a different view of citizens' rights, and political participation in general. Citizen's rights in Marx's schema included political and civil rights, and rights of democratic participation. Marx is appreciative of citizens rights because they could be exercised by individuals only as members of the community, and their content was 'participation in the community life', in the 'political life of the community', and the 'life of the state'. He supported freedom of speech, dissent, and organization as well as universal franchise because he admitted the possibility of achieving socialist transformation through the vote.[10]

Anthony Gidden's Theory of Citizenship

According to Anthony Gidden, theory of modern citizenship is based on class conflict of Marx and product of various social movements. There is a vivid description of Marx's thoughts and ideas in Anthony Gidden's theory. According to him, citizenship and democracy are both associated with the expansion of state sovereignty. He has propounded that the view point of citizenship is based upon class conflict. According to Marx, the achievement of rights of citizens is the result of constantly going on class conflict. It was the conflict of the bourgeoisie and feudal privileges, followed by the struggle of the working class against the bourgeoisie. The struggle between the bourgeoisie and feudalism led to the separation of the state from the economy and the establishment of civil and political rights. Also democracy was adopted as a means to protect the freedom and equality of the citizen.

Gidden has also said that in the western countries the civil and political rights acquired for the development of citizenship can not be separated. One type of rights also includes the other types of rights. Gidden does not look outside the four walls formed by Karl Marx. According to him most of the contemporary societies mainly the British society, was divided between the capitalist and working class. In such society the capitalist class had monopoly over the rights of the citizens and the working class is exploited by the capitalist class. Gidden says the use of political rights for the working class is impossible because they can not play the decisive role. Gidden always supported the Marxist ideology but later he realized that class conflict did not occur in all the European nations so in his next book, "Nation State and Violence" he rejected the numerous Marxist views.[11] He has said that in capitalist countries welfare capitalism has got established because of which the condition of working class has improved, many plans and policies were made to improve their welfare.

Gidden while explaining the establishment of welfare capitalism says that

> *"among the industrialized societies at least, capitalism is by now a very different from what it was in the nineteenth century and labour movements have played a prime role in changing it. In most of the capitalist countries, we have now to speak of the existence of 'welfare state', a system in which the labour movement has achieved a considerable stake and in which economic (social) citizenship rights brook large."*

(Anthony Gidden, as cited in Political Theory by Sushila Ramaswamy, p. 221)

Feminist Theory of Citizenship

The most notable development in the theory of citizenship is the emergence of feminist idea Women have been deprived of citizenship rights since the ancient times. Feminism contends that women's lacking in full citizenship is coming from the patriarchal view of the gender role assigned to men and women. The emphasis on self–reliance is based on the patriarchal notion that men should financially support the family, while the women would look after the household and care for the young, old and the sick and the elderly. This disallows women's not only in full participation in society as an individual but also as citizens they remain deprived of political processes as dependent on and subject to the decisions of male political leaders. Male dominance has been used to exclude women from political and economic decision making even in the areas that concern women's issues. This is a near universal practice that across the world women have been under-represented in the legislature, executive, judiciary or bureaucracy. Political activity is primarily considered as masculine activity.

Liberal feminism stresses on equal rights and equal access but ignores human interdependence that is integral to both families and politics. Wollstonecraft feminism has been concerned with how women can be treated as equal citizen along with men. Socialist feminism accept the idea of equal rights and equal access but stress more on the need to transcend class societies through revolutionary struggle, thus subordinating the women's question to realization of socialism. For the liberals and Marxists men and women are same and hence deserving equal treatment. Postmodernist feminists, like Young, emphasize on the differences that separated men from the women and the way these differences ought to be reconciled with claim of justice and equality. Young argues that the liberals and republicans are committed to an ideal of impartiality and reason which acts to the disadvantage of certain groups in society and she identified the women and ethnic minorities as oppressed categories

The primary objective of the liberal feminists has been to bring women into full rights of democratic citizenship. The liberal feminists envisage a future where legal, political, social and economic rights will be achieved and women will be on equal footing with men in all spheres and reject division of responsibilities based on gender. Citizenship involves virtues, relations and practices that are expressly political and more specifically, participatory and democratic. As long as feminist focus exclusively on social and economic questions relating to children, family, schools, work, wages, abortion, abuse, pornography, they do not articulate a political vision or address the problem of citizenship. it is only when they will emphasize on the intrinsic value of citizenship, rather than undertake active citizenship for the pursuit of social and economic concerns, that feminists can hope to achieve a truly distinctive politics of their own . this means considering citizenship as a continuous activity and good in itself.[12]

T.H. Marshall's Theory of Citizenship

One of the most popular theories on citizenship continues to be that by T. H. Marshall. His theory is found to be in practice in some form or the other in modern political system of democracy. In his influential account of the growth of citizenship in England, he states that the concept developed in a particular relationship of conflict and collusion with capitalism. Marshall's widely accepted definition of citizens as 'full membership of a community' attempted to outline the process through which it was achieved. In *citizenship and social class 1950,* Marshall distinguishes three stands or bundle of rights constituting citizenship, viz., civil, political and social. Civil rights broadly defined as 'rights necessary for individual freedom'. These include freedom of speech, assembly, movement, conscience, the right to equality before the law, to own property, enter into contracts and so forth. Civil rights are therefore rights exercised within civil society, and their existence depends upon the establishment of limited government, government that respects the autonomy of the individual. The provision of political rights required the development of universal suffrage, political equality and democratic government. These rights provide the individual with the opportunity to participate in political life. Finally Marshall identified a range of 'social rights' which guarantee the citizen a minimum social status. These rights are divers but, in Marshall's opinion, include the right to basic economic welfare, social security and what he described, rather vaguely, as the right 'to live the life of a civilized being according to the standards prevailing in society'. The provision of social rights requires the development of a welfare state and an extension of state responsibilities into economic and social life.[13]

For Marshall, the fullest expression of citizenship requires a liberal democratic welfare state. By guaranteeing civil, political, and social rights to all, the welfare state ensures that every member of the society feels like a full member of society, able to participate in and enjoy the common life of society. Where any of these rights are withheld or isolated, people will be marginalized and unable to participate. Marshall's emphasis is on the social services and the educational system. In the British context, these different dimensions of citizenship evolved gradually in the eighteenth, nineteenth and twentieth centuries. However, he also adds that these broad periods are not watertight compartments since these different components require different institutional supports and emerged at different historical period. In the feudal setup, the source of citizenship was the restricted basis of a society full of cleavages and the visible hierarchies. Subsequently, the nature of citizenship changes with conflict between different social institutions and also social groups.

The relationship and the interplay between citizenship and social class is Marshall's most important contribution to the theory of citizenship and here, in the British context, he notes the coincidence of the rise of modern citizenship with the rise of capitalism. Since the basis of citizenship is very different from the capitalistic ethos it is 'reasonable to expect that the impact of citizenship on social class should take the form of conflict between opposing principles'. What is striking is that the opposite evolution takes place without being contradictory and mutually exclusive. It is accepted that in the initial phase of the development of capitalism, citizenship undermines the privileges of the feudal elite while consolidating the capitalist class relation and divisions based on commodity production and exchange. Modern citizenship evolves out of limited formal basis of legal equality doing away with the feudal societal setup permitting the actualization of a new class system with the institution of private property. Paradoxically, citizenship initially does away with a particular class system and promotes another. However, in the eighteenth and nineteenth centuries citizenship rights co-existed harmoniously with the inequalities of the capitalist system as those rights are the basic requirements to maintain particular kind of inequality. During this period, citizenship rights are exclusively civil rights, which was the basic requirement of a competitive market economy. For entering the market, both the capitalist and the workers have the same perception of civil rights. Marshall argues that, if such rights are the basis of citizenship then inevitably citizenship strengthens and stratifies class inequalities. However, when citizenship incorporates political and social rights as well , then the conflict with the unequal class system actualized by civil rights leads to a situation of conflict.

Citizenship performs an integrative function, as by promoting equality of status of each individual it combats the disruptive inequalities of market economy. Equality of citizenship allows the acceptance of economic inequalities. Marshall agrees that even if citizenship can really overcome market inequality totally tension will always persist and integration will remain incomplete. This act of integration is not only a situation of equalizing rights for all but also a feeling of actual membership of the community. This realization is impossible in a feudal setup.

Marshall's theory of integration has three distinctive parts:

First, civil rights creates a citizenship in which distinct and particularistic class cultures decline, as graphically told by Shaw in Pygmalion, which has been made immortal and popular by its theatrical and cinematic versions called My Fair Lady.

Second, social rights drastically reduce class inequalities, with the majority of people identifying themselves as middle class.

Third, mass production provides the basis of a common material civilization, which in turn develops into an integrative citizenship.

Like civil rights, social movements are also important in Marshall's account of citizenship. Civil rights create groups, associations and movements of a wide variety and in the situation of a conspicuous absence of civil rights; social movements can be a source of power capacitating a group for effective action. Social movements play a dual role as contributing and facilitating citizenship.[14] Many thinkers also criticized the Marshall's theory of citizenship.

According to Antony Gidden, Marshall fails to emphasize that citizenship rights have been achieved in substantial degree only through the struggle. According to Gidden, the three fold classification is a gross overstatement and that Marshall simplifies the role of politics and the state in his theory. He acknowledges the support and approval of the state in consolidating citizenship but ignores the struggle of the people in achieving it as he believed that citizenship is the product of social movements.

Turner finds that Marshall's overemphasis and preoccupation with class had led to the neglect of other important factors of modern social change, mainly war and migration. Turner observes that, 'Marshall can be interpreted as saying that social violence has the potential for expanding the universalistic definition of the citizen'. Turner criticized Marshall for accepting the British nation state the way it is, but forgets that he gathers the historical antecedents from the same framework and analyzes it till the present without making any claim for the future. Turner mentions four waves of modern citizenship as an alternative to the historical evolution that Marshall suggests. These are: a) consequences of the removal of property connotation from definition of citizenship, b) removal of sex as a category, c) redistribution of age kingship and family for citizenship rights and d) expansion of citizenship rights by including nature and environment.[15] According to Derek Heater, Marshall's theory citizenship was temporally and geographically too myopic, his version of citizenship was too exclusive; vision was too optimistic; his triad of rights was too simplistic and interpretation was too unhistorical.

Can Citizenship be Acquired?

In modern political system there are provisions by which an individual can acquire citizenship. Apart from those who are naturalized citizens or whose ancestors have lived in the country for generations, there are also those who for various reasons seek citizenship status. Citizenship maybe acquired by marriage, adoption, long time residence, purchase of property and land, by way of contributing in the economic and social development, to name a few. Some countries also practice of conferring citizenship upon individuals of great achievement like intellectuals and scholars, artists or renowned public figures. In contemporary times people apply for citizenship through immigration laws that allow professionals and businessmen to relocate. In today's globalized world it is a common practice for people to migrate to different countries in search of better opportunities. There are laws in each country to be followed for such movements.

RIGHTS AND OBLIGATIONS

A citizen is someone who possesses rights, which are denied to the foreigners. In the liberal theory of citizenship certain rights have been guaranteed by the constitution to be honoured by the state. These are basic rights that allow a person to realize full individual growth by way of having access to various facilities and opportunities. The original meaning of the term right stood for a power or privilege as in the right of the nobility, the right of the clergy, and, of course, the divine right of the kings. In its modern sense, it refers to an entitlement to act or be treated in a particular way. Most modern thinkers have nevertheless been prepared to express their ideas in terms of rights or entitlements. Marshall divides citizenship rights into three categories: civil rights; political rights and social rights.

According to Marshall *Civil rights* is necessary for individual freedom, include freedom of speech, movement, conscience, the rights to equality before law, and the right to property. For Hayek and Nozick certain rights become negative rights in the context of welfare state as citizens become dependent on the state for social services entitled under the citizenship rights.

Political rights, viz, the right to vote, the right to stand for elections and the right to hold public office, provided the individual of political rights required the development of universal suffrage, political equality and democratic government.

Social rights guaranteed the individual a minimum social status and provided the basis for the exercise of both civil and political rights. These were 'positive' rights to live the life of civilized being according to the standards prevailing in society.

With the expansion of rights of citizenship, Marshall notes that, there was also an expansion of class of citizens. According to him, if any of these rights are violated, people will be marginalized and unable to participate. This theory is often called passive or private citizenship, because of its emphasis on passive entitlements, and the absence of any obligation to participate in public life as noted by the critics of his theory. Many commentators argue that we need to replace the passive acceptance of citizenship rights with the active exercise of citizenship responsibilities and duties, including economic self- reliance, political participation, and even civility. Marshall's view has also been criticized as narrow and homogenizing the character of citizenship an for failing to properly recognize and accommodate the social and cultural pluralism of modern societies.[16]

Theorists of citizenship were to specify more concretely the sorts of civic virtues required for a flourishing democracy. Along with the rights, duties of the citizens is equally important. Rights and duties are interrelated to each other as the right of one individual becomes the duty of another who has to honour or respect it. Some people think of citizenship only in terms of rights and do not give any importance to duties which rights impose on them. Rights are not possible without the duties.

Obligations of the citizens are classified in to four categories namely – moral obligations, legal obligations, positive obligations and negative obligations.

(i) Moral obligations: Moral obligation need not come from state institutions and be found outside the legal framework of the state. These obligations are inherent in the society as every society follows certain moral principles developed in the course of time based upon the history, culture and traditions of the society. Similarities and differences in moral principles maybe found among different societies including in the way the societies abide by these principles. Violation of moral obligations may lead to public criticism or social disapproval but there can be no legal punishment for such act of violations as there is no legal sanction behind it. These are the product of social consensus and public opinion is the sanction behind these obligations.

(ii) Legal obligations: The obligations prescribed by law and which are binding upon the individuals, are called legal obligations. Legal obligations are institutionalized and the duties of the citizen are prescribed by the law. There is the sanction of law behind the legal obligations. If anybody fails to discharge his legal duties properly, he will be punished by the law. These laws are for the purpose of objectively maintaining the smooth functioning of the state. For instance, it is the legal duty of the people to honestly pay their taxes to the state, failing of which he will be punished by the state. Most people perform their legal duties not due to the coercive power of the state, but due to their law- abiding nature and their realization that it is necessary in the larger interest of the society.

(iii) Positive obligations: All the people are expected to render certain services to the state for the benefit of the society or the state. While it is the responsibility of the state to undertake certain developmental activities to improve the condition of the society, it is the duty of citizens to participate in such projects as an equal partner. It is for the citizens to make such projects successful by contributing to generate resources in the form of taxes. The citizens as legally and morally bound members of the national community should also join various services for the development and betterment of the society at the various stations of life. The positive obligations are those obligations which are laid down by the law of the state, and there is the support of the state behind these obligations.

(iv) Negative obligations: Some of the obligations include responsibility to refrain from engaging in acts that go against the larger interest of the state and society. The law commands its citizens not to do certain things. The citizens should not involve in any activities which are likely to disturb peace and security of the country. These are called negative obligations. The citizens must avoid doing certain things which are prevented by the laws of the country.[17]

According to William Galston responsible citizenship requires four types of civic virtues:

(i) **General virtue** which is to do with individial's sense of courage, law-abidingness, commitment to cause, etc.

(ii) **Social virtue** is reflective of a citizen's independence and open-mindedness;

(iii) **Economic virtue** is related to work ethic; capacity to delay self gratification; adaptability to economic and technological change, responsible use of resources and

(iv) **Political virtue** that is the capacity to discern and respect the rights of others; willingness to demand only what can be paid for; ability to evaluate the performance of those in office; willingness to engage in public discourse.

Many of these virtues, particularly the general and economy virtues are needed in virtually any political order, whether it is large or small, agrarian or industrialized, democratic or authoritarian, pluralistic or homogeneous. For this reason, political thought, even when political communities were much smaller and more homogeneous. The civic virtues required for a large, pluralistic modern society, and the appropriate means to promote them, may differ from those required for a small, homogeneous pre-modern city state. These virtues include the ability and willingness to question political authority, and to engage in public discourse about matters of public policy. These are perhaps the most distinctive aspects of citizenship in a liberal democracy, since they are precisely what distinguish 'citizens' within a democracy from the 'subjects' of an authoritarian regime.[18]

Thomas Hobbes, in his Leviathan (1651) argued that citizens have an absolute obligation to obey political authority, regardless of how government may behave. In effect, Hobbes believed that though citizens were obliged to obey their state, the state itself was not subject to any reciprocal obligation. Because Hobbes believed that the existence of any state, however oppressive, is preferable to the existence of no state at all, which would lead to a descent into chaos and barbarism. For Hobbes, citizens are confronted by a stark choice between absolutism and anarchy.[19]

Citizenship as a binding principle makes itself manifest in civil society, 'the Setting of settings', which provides the space where individuals as part of diverse social groups are trained in civility and self-restraint. Theorists of the 'new right', however, see social rights as promoting passivity and a culture of dependency among the poor. Working within a framework of common good and common obligation of all citizens, they argue for a workfare programme instead of a welfare programme, cutting back the safety net of the poor, and tying welfare benefits to work responsibilities. Unlike the civil society theorists who argue for the enhancement of responsible citizenship through participation in institutions of civil society, the 'new right' sees the 'market' characterized by free trade, deregulation, tax-cuts, the weakening of trade unions, and the tightening of unemployment benefits, as the 'school' where citizenship 'virtues' of initiative, self reliance, and self sufficiency are learned.[20]

CIVIC CULTURE

The idea of a civic culture emerged in 1963, from a classic study entitled Civic Culture by Almond and Verba. *The Civic Culture* is one of the earliest studies to emphasize the importance of social behaviour in public sphere, adult political socialization and experiences and to show the relative weakness of childhood socialization. In this book *The Civic Culture: Political Attitudes and Democracy in Five Nations* 1963, Gabriel Almond and Sidney Verba clarifies the relationship between the attitudes of citizens and the functioning of modern democratic states in the U.S., Britain, Germany, Italy and Mexico. Three main dimensions of political culture are studied and compared in this research conducted knowledge of the political system, feelings toward the political system, and attitudes toward the self as a political actor.

Almond and Verba discussed the historical origins of the civic culture and the functions of the culture in the process of social change. They mainly analyzed and gave descriptions of the culture and of the role it plays in the maintenance of democratic political system. The civic culture is not the political culture that one finds described in civics textbooks, which prescribe the way in which citizens ought to act in a democracy. The norms of citizen behavior found in the texts stress the participant aspects of political culture. The democratic citizen is expected to be active in politics and to be involved. Furthermore, he is supposed to be rational in his approach to politics, guided by reason, not by emotion. He is supposed to be well informed and to make decisions - for instance, his decision on how to vote - on the basis of careful calculation as to the interests and the principles he would like to see furthered. This culture, with its stress on rational participation within the input structures of politics, we can label the "rationality-activist" model of political culture. The civic-culture shares much with this rationality-activist model; it is, in fact, such a culture plus something else.

There are some specific, characteristics in civic culture. The civic culture, for instance, exhibits participatory characteristics in which participatory action is based upon assumptions of rationality, and in such a way that "political culture and political structure are congruent". Moreover, the civic culture, with its emphasis upon rational participation in political life, combines with, rather than replaces, the "subject and parochial political orientations. The maintenance of these more traditional attitudes and their fusion with the participant orientations lead to a balanced political culture in which political activity, involvement, and rationality exist but are balanced by passivity, traditionality, and commitment to parochial values".[21] Pursuing the same theme, Inglehart finds that, among the polities of Europe, basic satisfaction with life and political circumstances, and levels of inter-personal trust, are strongly correlated with both the existence of relatively long-lived and stable democratic institutions, *and* with relative affluence of the populace. After examining economic, political, and cultural variables for several European policies over the twentieth century, Inglehart contends that "viable democracy does *not* depend on economic factors alone. Specific cultural factors are crucial, and they in turn are related to economic and macropolitical developments.... Stable democracy reflects the interaction of economic, political, *and* cultural factors".[22]

Almond and Verba described civic cultures as high frequencies of political activity, of exposure to political communications, of political discussion, of concern with political affairs. But there is something else.

In the first place, the civic culture is an allegiant participant culture. Individuals are not only oriented to political input. They also are oriented positively to the input structures and the input process. In other words, the civic culture is a participant political culture in which the political culture and political structure are congruent.

More important, in the civic culture participant political orientations combine with and do not replace subject and parochial political orientations. Individuals become participants in the political process, but they do not give up their orientations as subjects or as parochials. Furthermore, not only are these earlier orientations maintained, alongside the participant political orientations, but the subject and parochial orientations are also congruent with the participant political orientations. The non participant, more traditional political orientations tend to limit the individual's commitment to politics and to make that commitment milder. In a sense, the subject and parochial orientations "manage" or keep in place the participant's political orientations. Thus attitudes favorable to participation within the political system play a major role in the civic culture, but so do such nonpolitical attitudes as trust in other people and social participation in general.

Almond and Verba claim to have identified three broad types of political culture:

(1) ***parochial***, in which no clear differentiation of specific political roles and expectations exists among actors, i.e. "political specialization is minimal".

(2) ***subject***, in which institutional and role differentiation exists in political life, but towards which the citizen stands in largely passive relations; and

(3) ***participant***, in which the relationships between specialized institutions and citizen opinion and activity is interactive. They summarize this general schema as follows:

> "A participant is assumed to be aware of and informed about the political system in both its governmental and political aspects. A subject tends to be cognitively oriented primarily to the output side of government: the executive, bureaucracy, and judiciary. The parochial tends to be unaware, or only dimly aware, of the political system in all its aspects" .

Almond and Verba, and later, Inglehart, argue that if "a democratic political system is one in which the ordinary citizen participates in political decisions, a democratic political culture should consist of a set of beliefs, attitudes, norms, perceptions and the like, that support participation".[23] Moreover, associated with this participatory value-orientation is an assumption about the character of rational behaviour in participation, this as opposed to "emotional", sentiment-driven involvement.

PARTICIPATORY CITIZEN

For the last twenty years, the concept of .participation has been widely used in the discourse of development. The concept of participation is being related to rights of citizenship and to democratic governance. Participation in democracies should go beyond taking part in voting, and should include participation in governance processes. The notion of citizenship (especially in societies that are stratified) brings in several benefits to some groups and restricts the rights and freedoms of others, as it seldom accommodates completely people with lower status. Traditional notions of participation limit the participation of citizens to the voting processes in democracies and to their involvement with government-owned initiatives that provide services to groups which are of lesser sociopolitical or economic status.

The moves from government towards civil society, and from social and project participation towards governance offer new spaces in which the concept of participation may also be expanded to one of citizenship. One which involves linking participation in the political, community and social spheres. It also offers new opportunities to share the methods for strengthening participation across boundaries. So that, for instance, those who have been promoting participatory planning can learn lessons about advocacy or human rights education, and those who have developed participatory methods for consultation, planning and monitoring are able to link them to the new governance agenda.

The concept of citizenship has long been a disputed and value-laden one in democratic theory. To some, citizenship has implied a set of individual rights, while to others it is seen as a broader set of social and civic responsibilities. More recently, some have argued for linking these two traditions, such that the right of participation in decision-making in social, economic, cultural and political life should be included in the nexus of basic human rights. Citizenship as participation can be seen as representing an expression of human agency in the political arena, broadly defined; citizenship as rights enables people to act as agents.

It is necessary to improve opportunity for civil society organizations to enhance citizen participation, leading to more participatory democracies: "Civil society organizations have been constrained by the actions of most governments, and most of these organizations have first to create avenues wherein they can operate in a flexible manner, before making attempts to have a say in government affairs. Effective participation is also constrained by insufficient funds and so the scope and the mandate of networks are limited. Participatory citizenship calls for a renaissance in the relations between citizens and the state and this includes space for participation by representatives of citizens, networks, individuals with unique identities and other non-state actors."

SOCIAL AUDIT

Basis of Social Audit

Social audit as a term was used as far back as the 1950s. Though it is not directly reflective of rights and obligations of the citizens, it works to maintain the balance of power between state institutions, local civic bodies and citizens. Social audit is based on the principle that democratic local governance should be carried out, as far as possible, with the consent and understanding of all concerned. It is thus a process and not an event.

What is a Social Audit?

A social audit is a way of measuring, understanding, reporting and ultimately improving an organization's social and ethical performance. A social audit helps to narrow gaps between vision/goal and reality, between efficiency and effectiveness. It is a technique to understand, measure, verify, report on and to improve the social performance of the organization.

Social auditing creates an impact upon governance. It values the voice of stakeholders, including marginalized/poor groups whose voices are rarely heard. Social auditing is taken up for the purpose of enhancing local governance, particularly for strengthening accountability and transparency in local bodies.

The key difference between development and social audit is that a social audit focuses on the neglected issues of social impacts, while a development audit has a broader focus including environment and economic issues, such as the efficiency of a project or programme.

Objectives of Social Audit

1. Assessing the physical and financial gaps between needs and resources available for local development.

2. Creating awareness among beneficiaries and providers of local, social and productive services.

3. Increasing efficacy and effectiveness of local development programmes.

4. Scrutiny of various policy decisions, keeping in view stakeholder interests and priorities, particularly of rural poor.

5. Estimation of the opportunity cost for stakeholders of not getting timely access to public services.

Advantages of Social Audit

(a) Trains the community on participatory local planning;

(b) Encourages local democracy;

(c) Encourages community participation;

(d) Benefits disadvantaged groups;

(e) Promotes collective decision making and sharing responsibilities;

(f) Develops human resources and social capital.

To be effective, the social auditor must have the right to:

1. seek clarifications from the implementing agency about any decision-making, activity, scheme, income and expenditure incurred by the agency;
2. consider and scrutinize existing schemes and local activities of the agency; and
3. access registers and documents relating to all development activities undertaken by the implementing agency or by any other government department.

This requires transparency in the decision-making and activities of the implementing agencies. In a way, social audit includes measures for enhancing transparency by enforcing the right to information in the planning and implementation of local development activities.

SOCIAL AUDIT IN INDIA

Public Documents for Social Audit in India

There has been a flurry of activity and interest in the last seven to eight years in India and neighboring countries. Voluntary development organizations are also actively concerned.

(a) All budget allocations, beneficiary lists, muster rolls, bills, vouchers, accounts, etc. must be available for public scrutiny.

(b) All applications for licenses/permits and certificates issued by local self-government institutions must have a serial number. Registers indicating date of application and date of clearance in each case should be available for reference by any applicant. If possible, copies should be publicly displayed.

(c) Public assessment of tax, exemptions, grants, etc., to ensure there are no complaints of undue preferential treatment.

Several states have declared all *Gram Panchayat* plan documents related to beneficiary selection, budget cost estimates, etc. to be public documents. A daily notice to be posted at the site of all development works, lists names of workers, wages paid, cost and quantities of material, transport charges, etc.

However, social audit arrangements have mostly been ineffective because there is no legal provision for punitive action. States should enact legislation to facilitate social audit by the *Gram Sabha.*

Appropriate Institutional Level for Social Audit in India

In India the most appropriate institutional level for social audit is the *Gram Sabha,* which has been given 'watchdog' powers and responsibilities by the *Panchayati Raj* Acts in most States to supervise and monitor the functioning of *panchayat* elected representatives and government functionaries, and examine the annual statement of accounts and audit reports. These are implied powers indirectly empowering *Gram Sabhas* to carry out social audits in addition to other functions. Members of the *Gram Sabha* and the village *panchayat*, intermediate *panchayat* and district *panchayat* through their representatives, can raise issues of social concern and public interest and demand an explanation.

The *Gram Sabha* should have the mandate to: inspect all public documents related to budget allocations, list of beneficiaries, assistance under each scheme, muster rolls, bills, vouchers, accounts, etc., for scrutiny; examine annual statements of accounts and audit reports; discuss the report on the local administration of the preceding year; review local development for the year or any new activity programme; establish accountability of functionaries found guilty of violating established norms/rules; suggest measures for promoting transparency in identifying, planning, implementing, monitoring and evaluating relevant local development programmes; and ensure opportunity for rural poor to voice their concerns while participating in social audit meetings.

Right to information for members of Gram Sabha

Some States have already passed Right to Information Acts. Notwithstanding some weaknesses, the Acts have opened the way for transparency in administration from the State to the *panchayat* level.

The Right to Information Acts specify the modalities for obtaining information and provide penalties or failing to furnish or supplying false information. The Acts facilitate social legislation such as on minimum wages and gender rights and, more importantly, pave the way for public debate on government development projects.

However, none of the Acts have defined the right to information to include inspection of works and documents, and the taking of notes and extracts. This is needed to make the social audit by the *Gram Sabha* more effective.

Social Audit Committees

Social audit can also be used for auditing the performance of all three PRI tiers with a social audit committee at each level.

These committees should not be permanent, but can be set up depending on the nature of programmes/schemes to be audited.

Social audit committee members can be drawn from among programme stakeholders. It is advisable to use the services of retired functionaries of different organizations, teachers or persons of impeccable integrity living in the *Zilla Panchayat*/Block *Panchayat/Gram Panchayat* jurisdiction. Both facilitators and social audit committee members can be trained by social audit experts.

Steps in social audit in local bodies

1. Clarity of purpose and goal of the local elected body.

2. Identify stakeholders with a focus on their specific roles and duties. Social auditing aims to ensure a say for all stakeholders. It is particularly important that marginalized social groups, which are normally excluded, have a say on local development issues and activities and have their views on the actual performance of local elected bodies.

3. Definition of performance indicators which must be understood and accepted by all. Indicator data must be collected by stakeholders on a regular basis.

4. Regular meetings to review and discuss data/information on performance indicators.

5. Follow-up of social audit meeting with the *panchayat* body reviewing stakeholders' actions, activities and viewpoints, making commitments on changes and agreeing on future action as recommended by the stakeholders.

6. Establishment of a group of trusted local people including elderly people, teachers and others who are committed and independent, to be involved in the verification and to judge if the decisions based upon social audit have been implemented.

7. The findings of the social audit should be shared with all local stakeholders. This encourages transparency and accountability. A report of the social audit meeting should be distributed for *Gram Panchayat* auditing. In addition, key

decisions should be written on walls and boards and communicated orally.

Key factors for successful social audit

- Level of information shared with and involvement of stakeholders, particularly of the rural poor, women, and other marginalized sections.
- Commitment, seriousness and clear responsibilities for follow-up actions by elected members of the *Gram Panchayat.*
- Involvement of key facilitators in the process.[24]

CITIZEN POLICING

Community Policing

It is a concept that refers to policing practice aiming to increase interaction between citizens and police officials for public safety and quality of life in the community. It is conceived with an objective to bring about a change in the way policing is done. It has become the national mantra to spring up in urban, suburban, and even rural police departments or police stations. The CP promises to change relationships progressively to improve the living conditions of neighborhoods and for reducing crime in the community.

There is no one commonly recognized definition of community policing, and there is an un cautious tendency to label anything and everything as community policing. However, a good working definition would be "a department-wide *philosophy* of *full-service*, *personalized* and *decentralized* policing, where citizens feel *empowered* to work in *proactive partnerships* with the police at *solving* the *problems* of crime, fear of crime, disorder, decay, and quality of life."[25] Community policing encourages the use of non-law enforcement resources within a law enforcement agency such as volunteerism, which involves active citizen participation with their law enforcement agency. Volunteer efforts can help free up officer time, and provide an effective channel for citizen input. It has long been recognized that many of the basic functions within a law enforcement agency can be accomplished by other than sworn deputies or civilian employees. Volunteer efforts can help free up officer time, and allow sworn personnel to be more proactive and prevention-oriented. In many countries, citizens who have the time to volunteer in the community have offered their services to law enforcement agencies, freeing up law enforcement personnel to spend more time in a crime reduction role.

There are different aspects of citizen policing such as neighborhood watch, volunteers in Police Service (VIPS), Community volunteers for disaster management and community Medical services, all of which integrate well with the community policing philosophy. In fact, Neighborhood Watch has been an integral component of the community policing philosophy virtually since its inception.

The concept of community policing emerged in some states of India as a result of growing social and communal unrest. The need to maintain vigilance in the aftermath of communal riots was one of the reasons for the birth of the concept where members of some communities formed groups for the security of the community people. For example, Prahari, a community policing initiative in Assam, Trichy Community Policing, Samarth Yojna Community Policing Experiment in Coimbatore city, Friends of Police in Tamil Nadu and Public Concern for Governance Trust for Mumbaites.[26]

Some of the elements of community policing are:

Neighborhood Watch

It becomes important for citizens to participate in policing and crime prevention programs formally or informally organized either by state institutions or voluntary bodies. These programmes engages volunteer citizen action to enhance security within local communities by encouraging citizens to report suspicious activity in their immediate neighborhoods to the police. In addition to serving a crime prevention role, Neighborhood Watch can also be used as the basis for bringing neighborhood residents together to focus on disaster preparedness as well as terrorism awareness, to focus on evacuation drills and exercises, and even to organize group training, such as the Community Emergency Response Team (CERT) training as found in the US of America.

Volunteers in Police Service (VIPS)

This program provides training for civilian volunteers who assist local police departments by performing "non-sworn" duties, effectively freeing up officers to spend more time on critical functions. This concept was developed in America since September 11, 2001, as the demands on state and local law enforcement have increased dramatically. Such programmes play crucial role during emergency times when already-limited resources are being stretched farther and every available state services have reached near exhaustion. The program provides resources to assist local law enforcement officials by incorporating community volunteers into the activities of the law enforcement agency and by using best practices to help state and local law enforcement design strategies to recruit, train, and utilize citizen volunteers in their departments.

Community volunteers for disaster management

In times of natural calamities like earthquake, tsunami, flood, draught, the state alone can not reach out to the ones affected and has to depend largely on local communities. There are non-government voluntary organizations who participate alongside government agencies to carry relief aids to the people under such conditions. Such organizations provide civilians with training in emergency management, planning and response functions to bolster the capacity of local communities to respond to disasters. When emergencies happen, members can give critical support to first responders, provide immediate assistance to victims, and organize spontaneous volunteers at a disaster site. Members can also help with non-emergency projects that help improve the safety of the community.

Community Medical Services

Community medical services are important in the context of bringing medical facilities to the people. They coordinate with the skilled medical practitioners and retired physicians, nurses, and other health professionals as well as other citizens interested in health issues who are eager to volunteer to address their community's ongoing public health needs and to help their community during large-scale emergency situations. Local community leaders develop their own medical centres and also identify the duties of the volunteers according to specific community needs. For example, in the US, Medical Reserve Corps (MRC) volunteers may deliver necessary public health services during a crisis, assist emergency response teams with patients, and provide care directly to those with less serious injuries and other health-related issues. The MRC plays an integral part in the preparedness and response strategy. It provides an organized way for medical and public health volunteers to offer their skills and expertise during local crises and throughout the year.

CIVIL SOCIETY

In any functioning democratic system the role of civil society can not be undermined. Civil society is a "space" that create possibilities of communication, interaction and cooperation between the state and the people. These bodies function as a mediator between the individual, community and the state distinguishes it from the government and the business sector. The members of the civil society are enlightened and active citizens with a vision to improve the living condition of the people, to help government administer, keep a vigil on the government functionaries, advocate socio-economic growth by promoting education and other citizen related issues. While scholars debate the definition of civil society, they more or less agree that it comprises institutions such as religious organizations, labor unions, charities, community groups, nonprofits, and the media. In a healthy democracy these institutions supplement formal processes such as voting and help citizens shape the culture, politics, and economies of their nation.

It also uses various forums and instruments like the RTI and RTE to extract information and use this information to create awareness against undemocratic acts. The civil society is largely united against human rights violation, oppression, autocracy despite differences in opinion on various other matters. Hence, civil society's role is vital and effective. Education is a strong weapon that the civil society owns. The civil society is a watchdog of democracy. Exercising its freedom of expression, the civil society brings to light any oppressive move of the government or denial of democratic rights by government agencies.

Civil society also has an important role to play in development and aid effectiveness. It has been a strong advocate of changes in the way donors provide development assistance, and is an active partner around the Paris Declaration and Accra Agenda for Action.[27]

Many civil society organizations (CSOs) have a proven capacity for broad-based mobilization and creating bottom-up demand that fosters responsive governance. Civil society advocacy can facilitate the participation of poor and vulnerable populations in the design and implementation of development policies and programmes. This can enhance the delivery of basic social services, such as health and education. Civil society organizations also play a critical watchdog role in public life. Last but not least, members of civil society organizations volunteer their time, skills, and expertise to development.[28]

Core Ingredients of Civil Society

Governance is the process by which a society manages itself through the mechanism of the state. The core ingredients of good governance are:

People's effective participation, transparency, responsiveness, consensus orientation, equity and inclusiveness, the rule of law, effectiveness and efficiency, accountability, and strategic vision. These are crucially value-laden and constitute the bedrock of democracy.

Innumerable administrative reform commissions have produced no appreciable impact on the quality of governance. The emphasis now is on facilitating external pressure from citizens on the system to improve through the Right to Information Act, Consumer Protection Act, Citizens Charters, Whistleblower protection, e-governance, Report Cards, Democratic Decentralisation, Public Interest Litigation, etc.

Governance has three levels — internal systems and procedures; cutting edge systems and procedures; and check-and-balance systems at level (a) civil society can influence policy and project formulation through membership of committees, submission of memoranda directly or through elected representatives, and interactive rule-making in the implementation of policies, projects and schemes affecting citizens. The maximum day-to-day interaction between the government and the citizens takes place and the popular image of governance is formed at level (b) interactions of civil society with level (c) infrequent but important, will be more of an exposure of irregularities rather than steps for improvement in the quality of governance.

Civil society's functional contribution to good governance could be:

- **Watchdog** – against violation of human rights and governing deficiencies.
- **Advocate** – of the weaker sections' point of view.
- **Agitator** – on behalf of aggrieved citizens.
- **Educator** – of citizens on their rights, entitlements and responsibilities and the government about the pulse of the people.
- **Service provider** – to areas and people not reached by official efforts or as government's agent.
- **Mobiliser** – of public opinion for or against a programme or policy.

Civil society acts through 'social capital'– the capacity of people to act together willingly in their common long-term interest. Social capital is strong in a homogeneous, egalitarian society. Civil society as a whole is, therefore, unable to play its full potential role in enforcing good governance in India except when extraordinary leadership overcomes narrow loyalties, or when an issue is of common, major concern to all sections (like natural calamities). Smaller units of governance and decentralization of governance are, therefore, indispensable in India.

Individuals cannot take on the huge political-bureaucratic machine that the government is, nor can the entire civil society act on behalf of every citizen. Civil society, therefore, has to operate through compact, focused organizations based on strong social capital.

Efforts to improve the quality of governance will fail if the quality and caliber of the political executive is unsatisfactory. Civil society needs to note the deterioration in the quality, integrity and commitment of the elected representatives and the criminalization of politics. Voter education, electoral reforms and periodical highlighting of the performance (or non-performance) of elected representatives are high priority items in civil society's agenda. Parliamentary democracy becomes participative democracy only with civil society's active role.[29]

NOTES

1 Will Kymlicka, 2002. *Contemporary Political Philosophy: An Introduction*, Oxford University Press, p.287.

2 Anupama Roy, "Citizenship", in Rajeev Bhargava and Ashok Acharya (ed), 2008. *Political Theory: An Introduction,* Pearson Education, Delhi, pp. 132-134.

3 Sushila Ramaswamy, 2008. *Political Theory: An Idea and Concept,* Macmillan India Ltd, New Delhi, p.208.

4 Ibid p 208.

5 Anupama Roy, *Citizenship and Rights*. www.du.ac.in/fileadmn/du/academics/coursematerial

6 Sushila Ramaswamy, op.cit., pp., 211-212.

7 Ibid, p. 213.

8 R.C. Vermani, 2005. *An Introduction to Political Theory and Thought,* Gitanjali Publishing House, New Delhi, p. 94-95.

9 Ibid.

10 Anupama Roy, op.cit., p. 139.

11 Ibid.

12 Sushila Ramaswamy, op.cit., pp. 224-225.

13 Andrew Heywood, 2004. *Political Theory An Introduction,* Palgrave, New York, p. 207,

14 Sushila Ramaswamy op.cit., pp. 213-216

15 Ibid pp-217-219.

16 Will Kymlicka, op.cit., p. 287

17 H.H.Das and B.C. Chaudhury, 1999. *Political Theory*, Shree Mahavir Book Depot, Delhi, pp. 143-144.

18 Will Kymlicka, op.cit, pp.287-289.

19 Andrew Heywood, op.cit. p.199

20 Anupama Roy, Citizenship and Rights, *op.cit*

21 Almond and Verva, 1963. *The Civic Culture-Political Attitude and Democracy in five Nations,* Sage publication, pp.31-32.

22 Ibid.

23 Ibid, p. 178.

24 Report by K. B. Srivastava, former Professor and Head, Centre for *Panchayati Raj*, National Institute of Rural Development (NIRD), Hyderabad, India & Chandan Datta, PRIA, New Delhi.

25 Reports of homeland security and community policing, United state of America

26 http://www.humanrightsinitiative.org/new/community_policing_experiments_in_india_1.pdf)

27 (Amnesty International) *www.amnesty.org/en/united-nations/universal.../role-of-civil-societyý*

28 *www.undp.org/content/undp/en/home/.../civil_society_organizatio*

29 P.K. Doraiswamy, *The Role of Civil Society in Good Governance*, The Hindu, August 26, 2007.

REFERENCES

Barbalet, J.M. , 1988. *Citizenship: Rights, Struggle and Class Inequality*, University of Minnesota Press, Minneapolis.

Barbieri, William, 1998. *Ethics of Citizenship: Immigrants and Group Rights in Germany*, Duke University Press, Durham, NC.

Beiner, R, 1994. *Theorizing citizenship*, State University of New York Press, Albamy, NY.

Bulmer, Martin and Anthony Rees(eds), 1996. *Citizenship Today: The Contemporary Relevance of T.H.Marshall*, University College London Press, London.

Chandoke, Neera, 1995. *State and Civil Society: Exploration in Political Theory*, Sage Publication.

Clarke, P B, 1994. *Citizenship*, Pluto Press London.

Eamonn Callan, 1997. *Creating Citizens: Political Educatiomn and Liberal Democracy*, Oxford University Press, Oxford.

Heater, D, 1999. *What is Citizenship*? Polity Press, Cambridge.

Oldfield, A, 1990. *Citizenship and Community: Civic Republicanism and the Modern World*, Routledge, London.

Kymlicka, Will, 1995. *Multicultural Citizenship: A Liberal Theory of Minority Rights*, Oxford University Press, Oxford.

Turner and P. Hamilton(eds), 1994. *Citizenship: Critical Concepts*, vol.2 Routledge, London.

3

LAW ENFORCEMENT AND ADMINISTRATION OF JUSTICE

DR. DEEPAK YADAV

(A) POLICING AND ENFORCEMENT OF LAWS

HISTORICAL BACKGROUND

A *police force* is a constituted body of persons empowered by the state to enforce the law, protect property, and limit disorder. Their powers include the legitimized use of force. The term is most commonly associated with police services of a state that are authorized to exercise the police power of that state within a defined legal or territorial area of responsibility. Police forces are often defined as being separate from military or other organizations involved in the defense of the state against foreign aggressors; however, gendarmerie are military units charged with civil policing.

Law enforcement, however, constitutes only part of policing activity. Policing has included an array of activities in different situations, but the predominant ones are concerned with the preservation of order. In some societies, in the late 18th and early 19th centuries, these developed within the context of maintaining the class system and the protection of private property. Some parts of the world may suffer from police corruption. The police force is usually a public sector service, meaning they usually get paid by the taxpayer.

---

* Assistant Professor, Deptt. of Political Science, Kalindi College, Univ. of Delhi

Alternative names for police force include constabulary, gendarmerie, police department, police service, crime prevention, protective services, law enforcement agency, civil guard or civic guard. Members may be referred to as police officers, troopers, sheriffs, constables, rangers, peace officers or civic/civil guards. Police of the Soviet-era Eastern Europe were (or are, in some cases, as in Belarus) called the *militsiya*. The Irish police are called the Garda Síochána ("guardians of the peace"); a police officer is called a *garda*. And although the word "police" comes from the Greek police *Astynomia*.

In Ancient Greece, publicly owned slaves were used by magistrates as police. In Athens, a group of 300 Scythian slaves (the "rod-bearers") was used to guard public meetings to keep order and for crowd control, and also assisted with dealing with criminals, handling prisoners, and making arrests. Other duties associated with modern policing, such as investigating crimes, were left to the citizens themselves.

In the Roman Empire, the Army, rather than a dedicated police organization, provided security. Local watchmen were hired by cities to provide some extra security. Magistrates such as *procurators fiscal* and *quaestors* investigated crimes. There was no concept of public prosecution, so victims of crime or their families had to organize and manage the prosecution themselves.

The first centrally organised police force was created by the government of King Louis XIV in 1667 to police the city of Paris, then the largest city in Europe. The royal edict, registered by the *Parlement* of Paris on March 15, 1667 created the office of *lieutenant général de police* ("lieutenant general of police"), who was to be the head of the new Paris police force, and defined the task of the police as "ensuring the peace and quiet of the public and of private individuals, purging the city of what may cause disturbances, procuring abundance, and having each and everyone live according to their station and their duties".

Gabriel Nicolas de la Reynie, founder of the first uniformed police force in the world.This office was first held by Gabriel

Nicolas de la Reynie, who had 44 *commissaires de police* (police commissioners) under his authority. In 1709, these commissioners were assisted by *inspecteurs de police* (police inspectors). The city of Paris was divided into 16 districts policed by the *commissioners*, each assigned to a particular district and assisted by a growing bureaucracy. The scheme of the Paris police force was extended to the rest of France by a royal edict of October 1699, resulting in the creation of lieutenants general of police in all large French cities and towns.

After the French Revolution, Napoléon I reorganized the police in Paris and other cities with more than 5,000 inhabitants on February 17, 1800 as the Prefecture of Police. On March 12, 1829, a government decree created the first uniformed police in France, known as *sergents de ville* ("city sergeants"), which the Paris Prefecture of Police's website claims were the first uniformed policemen in the world.

In 1737, George II began paying some London and Middlesex watchmen with tax monies, beginning the shift to government control. In 1749 Henry Fielding began organizing a force of quasi-professional constables known as the Bow Street Runners. The Macdaniel affair added further impetus for a publicly salaried police force that did not depend on rewards. Nonetheless, In 1828, there were privately financed police units in no fewer than 45 parishes within a 10-mile radius of London.

The word "police" was borrowed from French into the English language in the 18th century, but for a long time it applied only to French and continental European police forces. The word, and the concept of police itself, was "disliked as a symbol of foreign oppression" (according to *Britannica 1911*). Before the 19th century, the first use of the word "police" recorded in government documents in the United Kingdom was the appointment of Commissioners of Police for Scotland in 1714 and the creation of the Marine Police in 1798.

The basis for the modern police force was laid down by reformers at the turn of the 19th century, on the basis of

Benthamite philosophy. In 1797, Patrick Colquhoun was able to persuade the West Indies merchants who operated at the Pool of London on the River Thames, to establish a police force at the docks to prevent rampant theft that was causing annual estimated losses of £500,000 worth of cargo.The idea of a police, as it then existed in France, was considered an affront to the liberal English. In building the case for the police in the face of England's firm anti-police sentiment, Colquhoun framed the political rationale on economic indicators to show that a police dedicated to crime prevention was "perfectly congenial to the principle of the British constitution." Moreover, he went so far as to praise the French system, which had reached "the greatest degree of perfection" in his estimation.

Law Enforcement in India

Prior to Independence, senior police officers belonging to the Imperial Police (IP) were appointed by the Secretary of State on the basis of a competitive examination.The first open civil service examination for admission to the service was held in England in June 1893 and the ten top candidates were appointed as probationers in the Indian (Imperial) Police. It is not possible to pinpoint an exact date on which the Indian Police came formally into being. Around 1907, the Secretary of State's officers were directed to wear the letters "IP" on their epaulettes in order to distinguish them from the other officers not recruited by the Secretary of State through examination. In this sense, 1907 could be regarded as the starting point.[1] In 1948, a year after India gained independence; the Imperial Police was replaced by IPS

The *Police Act of 1861* remains the central piece of legislation that governs all aspects of policing in India. Much of police work is also administered by the Indian Penal Code (IPC), the Code of Criminal Procedure (Cr.P.C) and the Indian Evidence Act 1872. The 1861 Act was established directly after the Indian Mutiny of 1857. The experience of such firm resistance led the colonial rulers to impose a regime police force upon their subjects, which could be used solely to consolidate and perpetuate their rule in the country. In fact, the 1861 Act instituted a police system designed to be absolutely subservient to the executive and highly authoritarian. The managerial philosophy of the police hierarchy was based on distrust of the lower ranks.

The advent of Indian independence transformed the political system, but the police system retained its colonial underpinnings. The Police Act of 1861 was not replaced. Political control over the police remained intact. Implanting mechanisms to assure accountability of the police to the public it serves did not become a priority, as it should have. The managerial philosophy, value system, and ethos of the police remained militaristic in design, and suppressive in practice. To this day, the police system in India can be characterized as a regime force, which places the needs of politicians or powerful individuals over the demands of the rule of law and the needs of citizens.

The years after independence witnessed the enactment of new legislation in several states of the country. The first to come into force was the Bombay Police Act of 1951, which also governs the police forces in Maharashtra and Gujarat. Next came the Kerala Police Act of 1960, followed by the Karnataka Police Act of 1963, and lastly the Delhi Police Act of 1978. Most recently, the government of Madhya Pradesh framed a Police Bill, 2002. Unfortunately, these new Acts were patterned almost exactly on the model of the 1861 Act, resulting in no significant improvement in the performance or behaviour of the police forces. In fact, some of these state Acts tightened political control even further over the police force, without introducing any safeguards to prevent misuse of the police for partisan purposes, or creating effective mechanisms to ensure police accountability.

(a) Indian Police Service (*IPS*)

The First Police Commission, appointed on 17 August 1865, contained detailed guidelines for the desired system of police in India and defined the police as a governmental department to maintain order, enforce the law, and to prevent and detect crime.

The Indian Police Service is not a force itself but a service providing leaders and commanders to staff the state police and all-India Central Armed Police Forces. Its members are the senior officers of the police. The Indian Police Service or **IPS**, is one of the three All India Services of the Government of India. In 1948, a year after India gained independence from Britain, the Indian (Imperial) Police, was replaced by the Indian Police Service. With the passage of time Indian Police Service's objectives were updated and redefined, the current rules and functions of an Indian Police Service Officer are as follows:

- To fulfill duties based on border responsibilities, in the areas of maintenance of public peace and order, crime prevention, investigation, and detection, collection of intelligence, VIP security, counter-terrorism, border policing, railway policing, tackling smuggling, drug trafficking, economic offences, corruption in public life, disaster management, enforcement of socio-economic legislation, bio-diversity and protection of environmental laws etc.
- Leading and commanding the Indian Intelligence Agencies like Research and Analysis Wing (R&AW), Intelligence Bureau (IB), Central Bureau of Investigations (CBI), Criminal Investigation Department (CID) etc., Indian Federal Law Enforcement Agencies, Civil and Armed Police Forces in all the states and union territories.
- Leading and commanding the Central Armed Police Forces (CAPF) which include the Central Police Organisations (CPO) and Central Paramilitary Forces (CPF) such as Border Security Force (BSF), Central Reserve Police Force (CRPF), Indo-Tibetan Border Police (ITBP), National Security Guard (NSG), Central Industrial Security Force (CISF), Vigilance Organisations, Indian Federal Law Enforcement Agencies.
- Serve at head of the departments in policy making in the Ministries and Departments of Central and State Governments and public sector undertakings both at centre and states, Government of India.
- To interact and coordinate closely with the members of other All India Services and with the elite Indian Revenue Service and

also with the Indian Armed Forces primarily with the Indian Army.

- Last but not the least, to lead and command the force with courage, uprightness, dedication and a strong sense of service to the people.
- Endeavour to inculcate in the police forces under their command such values and norms as would help them serve the people better.
- Inculcate integrity of the highest order, sensitivity to aspirations of people in a fast-changing social and economic milieu, respect for human rights, broad liberal perspective of law and justice and high standard of professionalism.

(b) State Police

Each state and union territory of India has a state police force, headed by the Commissioner of Police (State) or Director General of Police (DGP). Each state is controlled by the Chief Minister and Home Minister. The state police is responsible for maintaining law and order in townships of the state and the rural areas.

States such as West Bengal, Kerala, Tamil Nadu and Maharashtra have taken steps to get their police force trained by advanced police training schools notably the Scotland Yard, Atlanta City Police of the USA and the World Police Academy of Canada. The Tamil Nadu state police is at the forefront of advancement with the Tamil Nadu Police Academy which now is seeking university status. Kerala Police is also the first police force in South Asia, to adopt community policing for effective and pro-public friendly initiatives and action.

The Police Act of 1861 established the fundamental principles of organisation for police forces in India, and, with minor modifications, continues in effect. Consequently, although state-level police forces are separate and may differ in terms of the quality of equipment and resources, their patterns of organisation and operation are markedly similar.

A Director-general or inspector general, answerable to the home secretary of the state, heads each state, union territory, or national capital territory police force. Under the inspector general are a number of police "ranges" composed of three to six districts, headed by deputy inspectors general. District police headquarters are commanded by superintendents. District superintendents have wide discretionary powers and are responsible for overseeing subordinate police stations as well as specialty elements, such as criminal investigation detachments, equipment storehouses and armouries, and traffic police. Many large districts also have several assistant district superintendents.

Most preventive police work is carried out by constables assigned to police stations. Depending on the number of stations there, a district may be subdivided and, in some states, further divided into police "circles" to facilitate the supervision from district headquarters. Most of the major metropolitan areas such as New Delhi, Bombay, Calcutta, and Madras have separate municipal forces headed by commissioners. Police in the states and union territories are assisted by units of volunteer Home Guards, maintained under guidelines formulated by the Ministry of Home Affairs.

In most states and territories, police forces are functionally divided into civil (unarmed) police and armed contingents. The former, staffs police stations, conduct investigations, answer routine complaints, perform traffic duties, and patrol the streets. They usually carry lathis—bamboo staffs weighted or tipped with iron.

Contingents of armed police are divided into two groups, the district armed police and the Provincial Armed Constabulary. The district armed police are organised along the lines of an army infantry battalion. They are assigned to police stations and perform guard and escort duties. Those states that maintain distinct armed contingents employ them as a reserve strike force for emergencies. Such units are organised either as a mobile armed force under direct state control or in the case of district armed police (who are not as well equipped) as a force directed by district superintendents and generally used for riot-control duty.

The Provincial Armed Constabulary (Pradeshik) is an armed reserve maintained at key locations in some states and active only on orders from the deputy inspector general and higher-level authorities. Armed constabulary are not usually in contact with the public until they are assigned to VIP duty or assigned to maintain order during fairs, festivals, athletic events, elections, and natural disasters. They may also be sent to quell outbreaks of student or labour unrest, organised crime, and communal riots; to maintain key guard posts; and to participate in antiterrorist operations. Depending on the type of assignment, the Provincial Armed Constabulary may carry only lathis.

At all levels, the senior police officers answer to the police chain of command and respond to the general direction and control of designated civilian officials. In the municipal force, the chain of command runs directly to the state home secretary rather than to the district superintendent or district officials.

Working conditions and pay are poor, especially in the lower echelons of the police forces. Recruits receive only around₹, 9000 per month (about US$150). Opportunities for promotion are limited because of the system of horizontal entry into higher grades. Allegations of bribery, attributable to the low pay and poor working conditions, have been widespread.

Since the late 1980s, women have entered in larger numbers into the higher echelons of the Indian police, mostly through the Indian Police Service system. Women police officers were first used in 1972, and a number of women hold key positions in various state police organisations. However, their absolute numbers, regardless of rank, are small. Uniformed and undercover women police officers have been deployed in New Delhi as the Anti-Eve Teasing Squad, which combats sexual harassment against women ("Eves"). Several women-only police stations have also been established in Tamil Nadu to handle sex crimes against women.

Police uniforms vary widely according to grade, region, and kind of duty performed. Among the armed police, uniforms tend to resemble army dress rather than conventional police uniforms.

The khaki uniforms of the Indian Police Service officers are similar in all states, but headgear varies widely, especially among metropolitans areas.

(B) AUTONOMY AND NEUTRALITY OF INVESTIGATING AND ENFORCEMENT AGENCIES:

Autonomy and neutrality of investigating and enforcement agencies has been a major cause of concern world over. Many a times it has been blamed that government of day always tries to influence the investigating process to its own benefit. Functions and organizational structure of some of the main investing agencies in India are given bellow-

Central Bureau of Investigation (CBI)

The Central Bureau of Investigation (CBI) is the foremost investigating police agency in India, an elite force which plays a role in public life and ensuring the health of the national economy. It is under the jurisdiction of the Government of India. The CBI is involved in major criminal probes, and is the Interpol agency in India. The CBI was established in 1941 as the Special Police Establishment, tasked with domestic security. It was renamed the Central Bureau of Investigation on 1 April 1963. Its motto is "Industry, Impartiality, and Integrity".

Agency headquarters is in the Indian capital, New Delhi, with field offices located in major cities throughout India (including Mumbai). The CBI is overseen by the Department of Personnel and Training of the Ministry of Personnel, Public Grievances and Pensions of the Union Government, headed by a Union Minister who reports directly to the Prime Minister. While analogous in structure to the FBI, the CBI's powers and functions are limited to specific crimes by Acts (primarily the Delhi Special Police Establishment Act, 1946). The current CBI director is Ranjit Sinha.

The CBI is headed by a director, an IPS officer with a rank of Director General of Police or Commissioner of Police (State). The director is selected based on the CVC Act 2003, and has a two-year term. Other ranks in the CBI which may be staffed by the IPS or the IRS are Special director, Additional director, Joint director, Deputy inspector general of police, Senior superintendent of police and Superintendent of police. Additional superintendent of police, Deputy superintendent of police, Inspector, Sub-inspector, assistant sub-inspector, head constable, senior constable and Constable are recruited through SSC or through deputation from Police and Income Tax Departments.

The CBI is subject to five ministries of the Government of India:

1. Ministry of Home Affairs: Cadre clearance
2. Do PT: Administration, budget and induction of non IPS officers
3. Union Public Service Commission: Officers above the rank of Deputy SP
4. Law and Justice Ministry: Public prosecutors
5. Central Vigilance Commission: Anti-corruption case

The legal powers of investigation of the CBI are derived from the DSPE Act 1946, which confers powers, duties, privileges and liabilities on the Delhi Special Police Establishment (CBI) and officers of the Union Territories. The central government may extend to any area (except Union Territories) the powers and jurisdiction of the CBI for investigation, subject to the consent of the government of the concerned state. Members of the CBI at or above the rank of sub-inspector may be considered officers in charge of police stations. Under the act, the CBI can investigate only with notification by the central government.

Maintaining law and order is a state responsibility as "police" is a State subject, and the jurisdiction to investigate crime lies with the state police exclusively. The CBI being a Union subject may investigate:

- Offenses against central-government employees, or concerning affairs of the central government and employees of central public-sector undertakings and public-sector banks
- Cases involving the financial interests of the central government

- Breaches of central laws enforceable by the Government of India
- Major fraud or embezzlement; multi-state organized crime
- Multi-agency or international cases.

The High Courts and the Supreme Court have the jurisdiction to order a CBI investigation into an offense alleged to have been committed in a state without the state's consent, according to a five-judge constitutional bench of the Supreme Court (in Civil Appeals 6249 and 6250 of 2001) on 17 Feb 2010. The bench ruled:

> "*Being the protectors of civil liberties of the citizens, this Court and the High Courts have not only the power and jurisdiction but also an obligation to protect the fundamental rights, guaranteed by Part III in general and under Article 21 of the Constitution in particular, zealously and vigilantly.*"

The court clarified that this is an extraordinary power which must be exercised sparingly, cautiously and only in exceptional situations.

CBI is exempted from the provisions of the Right to Information Act. This exemption was granted by the government on 9 June 2011 (with similar exemptions to the National Investigating Agency (NIA), the Directorate General of Income Tax Investigation and the National Intelligence Grid (Natgrid)) on the basis of national security. It was criticized by the Central Information Commission and RTI activists, who said the blanket exemption violated the letter and intent of the RTI Act. The exemption was upheld in Madras High Court.

CRITICISM OF CBI

The functioning of CBI has always been criticized especially when powerful people are involved. India has seen many cases of corruption and misuse of power after independence which never reached on its conclusion. Some of the controversial cases mishandled by CBI are given below-

1. Corruption

Because of the CBI's political overtones, it has been exposed by former officials such as Joginder Singh and B. R. Lall (director and joint director, respectively) as engaging in nepotism, wrongful prosecution and corruption. In Lall's book, *Who Owns CBI*, he details how investigations are manipulated and derailed. Corruption within the organization has been revealed in information obtained under the RTI Act, and RTI activist Krishnanand Tripathi has alleged harassment from the CBI to save itself from exposure via RTI.

2. Political interference

Normally, cases assigned to the CBI are sensitive and of national importance. It is standard practice for state police departments to register cases under its jurisdiction; if necessary, the central government may transfer a case to the CBI. The agency has been criticised for its mishandling of several scams.It has also been criticized for dragging its feet investigating prominent politicians, such as P. V. Narasimha Rao, Jayalalithaa, Lalu Prasad Yadav, Mayawati and Mulayam Singh Yadav; this tactic leads to their acquittal or non-prosecution.[23]

3. Bofors scandal

In January 2006 it was discovered that the CBI had quietly unfrozen bank accounts belonging to Italian businessman Ottavio Quattrocchi, one of those accused in the 1986 Bofors scandal which tainted the government of Rajiv Gandhi.The CBI was responsible for the inquiry into the Bofors case. Associates of then-prime minister Rajiv Gandhi were linked to alleged payoffs made during the mid-1980s by Swedish arms firm AB Bofors, with US$40 million in kickbacks moved from Britain and Panama to secret Swiss banks. The 410 howitzers purchased in the US$1,300 million arms sale were reported to be inferior to those offered by a French competitor.

The CBI, which unfroze 21 crore (US$3.4 million) in a London bank in accounts held by Bofors, accused Quattrocchi and his wife Maria in 2006 but facilitated his travel by asking Interpol to take him off its wanted list on 29 April 2009. After communications from the CBI, Interpol withdrew the red corner notice on Quattrocchi.

4. Hawala scandal

A 1991 arrest of militants in Kashmir led to a raid on hawala brokers, revealing evidence of large-scale payments to national politicians. The Jain hawala case encompassed former Union ministers Ajit Kumar Panja and P. Shiv Shankar, former Uttar Pradesh governor Motilal Vora, Bharatiya Janata Party leader Yashwant Sinha. The 20 defendants were discharged by Special Judge V. B. Gupta in the 650-million case, heard in New Delhi.

The judge ruled that there was no *prima facie* evidence against the accused which could be converted into legal evidence. Those freed included Bharatiya Janata Party president L. K. Advani; former Union ministers V. C. Shukla, Arjun Singh, Madhavrao Scindia, N. D. Tiwari and R. K. Dhawan, and former Delhi chief minister Madan Lal Khurana. In 1997 a ruling by late Chief Justice of India J. S. Verma listed about two dozen guidelines which, if followed, would have ensured the independence of the investigating agency. Sixteen years later, successive governments circumvent the guidelines and treat the CBI as another wing of the government. Although the prosecution was prompted by a public-interest petition, the cases concluded with no convictions. In *Vineet Narayan & Othrs v Union of India AIR 1996 SC 3386*, the Supreme Court ruled that the Central Vigilance Commission should have a supervisory role over the CBI.

5. Priyadarshini Mattoo murder case

In this case Santosh Kumar Singh, the alleged murderer of a 22-year-old law student, was acquitted for what the judge called "deliberate inaction" by the investigating team. The accused was the son of a high-ranking officer in the Indian Police Service, the reason for the CBI's involvement. The 1999 judgment noted that "the influence of the father of the accused has been there".

Embarrassed by the judgment, CBI Director R. K. Raghavan appointed two special directors (P. C. Sharma and Gopal Achari) to study the judgement. The CBI appealed the verdict in Delhi High Court in 2000, and the court issued a warrant for the accused. The CBI applied for an early hearing in July 2006; in October the High Court found Singh guilty of rape and murder, sentencing him to death.

6. Sister Abhaya

This case concerns the 27 March 1992 death of a nun who was found in a water well in the Saint Pius X convent hostel in Kottayam, Kerala. Five CBI investigations have failed to yield any suspects.

7. Sohrabuddin case

The CBI has been accused of supporting the ruling Congress Party against its opposition, the BJP. The CBI is investigating the Sohrabuddin case in Gujarat; Geeta Johri, also investigating the case, claimed that the CBI is pressuring her to falsely implicate former Gujarat minister Amit Shah.

8. Sant Singh Chatwal case

Sant Singh Chatwal was a suspect in CBI records for 14 years. The agency had filed two charge sheets, sent letters rogatory abroad and sent a team to the US to imprison Chatwal and his wife from 2–5 February 1997. On 30 May 2007 and 10 August 2008 former CBI directors Vijay Shankar and Ashwani Kumar, respectively, signed no-challenge orders on the imprisonment. Later, it was decided not to appeal their release.

This closed a case of bank fraud in which Chatwal had been embroiled for over a decade. Along with four others, Chatwal was charged with being part of a "criminal conspiracy" to defraud the Bank of India's New York branch of 28.32 crore (US$4.5 million). Four charges were filed by the CBI, with Chatwal named a defendant in two. The other two trials are still in progress. RTI applicant Krishnanand Tripathi was denied access to public information concerning the closed cases. The

Central Information Commission later ordered the CBI to disclose the information; however, the CBI is exempt from the RTI Act. Chatwal is a recipient of the Padma Bhushan.

9. Malankara Varghese murder case

This case concerns the 5 December 2002 death of T. M. Varghese (also known as Malankara Varghese), a member of the Malankara Orthodox Church managing committee and a timber merchant. Varghese Thekkekara, a priest and manager of the Angamali diocese of the rival Jacobite Syrian Christian Church (part of the Syriac Orthodox Church), was charged with murder and conspiracy on 9 May 2010. Thekkekara was not arrested after he was charged, for which the CBI was criticised by the Kerala High Court and the media.

10. Bhopal gas tragedy

The CBI was publicly seen as ineffective in trying the 1984 Bhopal disaster case. Former CBI joint director B. R. Lall has said that he was asked to remain soft on extradition for Union Carbide CEO Warren Anderson and drop the charges (which included culpable homicide). Those accused received two-year sentences.

11. 2G spectrum scam

The UPA government allocated 2G spectrum to corporations at very low prices through corrupt and illegal means. The Supreme Court cited the CBI many times for its tardiness in the investigations;only after the court began monitoring its investigations were high-profile arrests made.

12. Indian coal allocation scam

This is a political scandal concerning the Indian government's allocation of the nation's coal deposits to private companies by Prime Minister Manmohan Singh, which cost the government 10673.03 billion (US$170 billion). CBI director Ranjit Sinha submitted an affidavit in the Supreme Court that the coal-scam status report prepared by the agency was shared with Congress Party law minister Ashwani Kumar "as desired by him" and with secretary-level officers from the prime minister's office (PMO) and the coal ministry before presenting it to the court.

NATIONAL INVESTIGATION AGENCY (NIA)

National Investigation Agency (NIA) is a federal agency established by the Indian Government to combat terror in India. It acts as the Central Counter Terrorism Law Enforcement Agency. The agency is empowered to deal with terror related crimes across states without special permission from the states. The Agency came into existence with the enactment of the National Investigation Agency Act 2008 by the Parliament of India on 31 December 2008.

The National Investigation Agency aims to be a thoroughly professional investigative agency matching the best international standards. The NIA aims to set the standards of excellence in counter terrorism and other national security related investigations at the national level by developing into a highly trained, partnership oriented workforce. NIA aims at creating deterrence for existing and potential terrorist groups/individuals. It aims to develop as a storehouse of all terrorist related information.

NIA was created after the 2008 Mumbai terror attacks as need for a central agency to combat terrorism was realised. The founding Director-General of NIA was Radha Vinod Raju, and he served till 31 January 2010. He was succeeded by Sharad Chandra Sinha till March 2013 when he was appointed the member of the National Human Rights Commission of India. In July 2013, Sharad Kumar was appointed as the Chief of National Investigation Agency succeeded by N R Wasan.

A Bill for the formation of the National Investigation Agency was passed by Parliament in December 2008. As per the Bill, NIA has concurrent jurisdiction which empowers the Centre to probe terror attacks in any part of the country, covering offences, including challenge to the country's sovereignty and integrity, bomb blasts, hijacking of aircraft and ships, and attacks on nuclear installations.

The ground staff of the agency in the national capital could be drawn from existing central staff and security organisations while in the states, permanent deputation from the state police could be taken. Other than offenses of terrorism, it also deals with counterfeit currency, human trafficking, narcotics or drugs, organised crime (extortion mobs and gangs), plane hijacking and violations of atomic energy act and weapons of mass destruction act.

The National Investigative Agency Bill and Unlawful Activities (Prevention) Amendment Bill on Tuesday, 30 Dec, 2008, became a law as President Pratibha Patil gave her assent to the legislation which was passed in the last session of Parliament.

Agency aims to be a thoroughly professional investigative agency matching the best international standards. It aims to set the standards of excellence in counter terrorism and other national security related investigations at the national level by developing into a highly trained, partnership oriented workforce. It also aims at creating deterrence for existing and potential terrorist groups/ individuals. It aims to develop as a storehouse of all terrorist related information.

The Agency has been empowered to conduct investigation and prosecution of offenses under the Acts specified in the Schedule of the NIA Act. A State Government may request the Central Government to hand over the investigation of a case to the NIA, provided the case has been registered for the offenses as contained in the schedule to the NIA Act. Central Government can also order NIA to take over investigation of any scheduled offense anywhere in the India. Officers of the NIA who are drawn from the Indian Revenue Service and the Indian Police Service have all powers, privileges and liabilities which the police officers have in connection with investigation of any offense.

Various Special Courts have been notified by the Central Government of India for trial of the cases registered at various police stations of NIA under Section 11 and 22 of the NIA Act 2008. Any question as to the jurisdiction of these courts is decided by the Central Government. These are presided over by a judge appointed by the Central Government on the recommendation of the Chief Justice of the High Court with jurisdiction in that region. Supreme Court of India has also been empowered to transfer the cases from one special court to any other special court within or outside the state if the same is in the interest of justice in light of the prevailing circumstances in any particular state. They are empowered with all powers of the court of sessions under Code of Criminal Procedure, 1973 for trial of any offense.

Trial by this courts are held on day-today basis on all working days and have precedence over the trial of any other case against the accused in any other court (not being a Special Court) and have to be concluded in preference to the trial of such other case. An appeal from any judgment, sentence or order, not being an interlocutory order, of a Special Court lies to the High Court both on facts and on law. Such an appeal is heard by a bench of two Judges of the High Court. At present there are 38 Special NIA Courts. State Governments have also been empowered to appoint one or more such special courts in their states.

In 2008, a fresh anti terrorism law came in the form of NIA. The crimes, related to security and integrity of country will treat as tackle because the new bill which has been passed by the government of India named National Investigation Agency Bill, 2008. NIA is an agency something like Central Bureau Investigation(CBI) but NIA has some compulsory & mandatory jurisdiction(sec[11] 6 and sec[12] 7) but CBI has no mandatory jurisdiction. In NIA no request is required but for CBI request should be made by state.

According to this enactment "the offence against the state" which are prescribed in chapter VI(sec 121-130) of land law, will directly treat NIA not local police. Not only this, offences related to Counterfeiting currency-notes or bank-notes (sec 489A-489E) also will be treating by this agency but it doesn't mean that in this march there in no role of local police. When any FIR is lodging with glimpse of eight scheduled offences in any police station then the duty officer will investigate that and send report to state government and they will forward to central and central govt. will decide, how to treat case?

Government ironically by this acts very much and gave steering of anti- terrorism in the hand of this. For this purpose, NIA officers will be given the magisterial powers to justify recording of confession before police as valid evidence against the accused. These are the crucial feature of this bill and these features are too beneficial to protect Indian security and this is examined by the some cases which have handed over to NIA. The reaction of home ministry was also positive with this as saying that, "Home Ministry sources say the proposed agency will be much more powerful than even the Federal Agency of the United States. They said a separate Bill will be moved in Parliament to amend the National Security Act of 1080 to constitute a National Security Authority that will supervise NIA investigations and permit prosecution of the culprits it nabs. The authority will have a senior IPS officer as security commissioner in each state for coordination of NIA with the state police".

BORDER SECURITY FORCE (BSF)

The Indian Border Security Force (BSF) is responsible for guarding India's land borders during peacetime and preventing trans-border crimes. It is a central police force operating under the Union Ministry of Home Affairs.

The Indo-Pakistani War of 1965 demonstrated the inadequacies of the existing border management system and led to the formation of the Border Security Force as a unified central agency with the specific mandate of guarding India's international boundaries. The BSF's policing capabilities were used in the Indo-Pakistani War of 1971 against the Pakistani Armed Forces in areas where the Indian Armed Forces was thinly spread; BSF troops took part in the Battle of Longewala.

BSF has own Tear Smoke Unit situated at BSF Academy, Takenpur, Gwalior (M P), which supplies to all state police forces for riot prevention. All state police (Maharashtra, GJ,UK, UP, RJ,J & K, TN, Punjab,Delhi,Bihar, WB, AP, HP etc. Police) have demand all Tear Smoke bomb and powder, which is used by their Vajra Vehicles and has also exported to foreign countries.

BSF is one of the Indian Police Force have his own Air Wing, Water Wing and also provides Choppers, Dogs and others useful service to all State Police. BSF have Dog Squad with National Dog Training and Research, Takenpur.

Although originally charged with guarding India's external boundaries, the BSF has more recently been given the task of aiding the Indian Army in counter-insurgency and counter-terrorism operations. When the insurgency in Jammu and Kashmir broke out in 1989, the Jammu and Kashmir state police and the thinly-deployed Central Reserve Police Force (CRPF) struggled to cope with the spiraling violence, and the Indian government deployed the BSF to Jammu and Kashmir to combat Islamic militants.

Central Industrial Security Force (CISF)

The Central Industrial Security Force (CISF) is used to guard industrial installations aroun`d the country owned by the Central government as well as securing seaports and airports. CISF also provides security to certain NGOs.

Central Reserve Police Force (CRPF)

The Central Reserve Police Force (CRPF) is one of the largest Central Police organisations in the world. Its main objective is to assist and help state and union territories' law enforcement agencies in maintaining law and order and to contain insurgency. It is also deployed as anti-terrorist unit in various regions. It is even operating abroad as part of United Nations peacekeeping missions. It is performing a variety of duties ranging from VIP security to election duties, from guarding of vital installations to the counter-naxal operations.

Indo-Tibetan Border Police (ITBP)

The Indo-Tibetan Border Police (ITBP) is one of the five main Central Armed Police Forces, responsible for security along the Indo-Tibetan Border, covering 2115 km. The ITBP personnel are trained in the fields of law & order, military tactics, jungle warfare, counter insurgency and internal security

ITBP is an elite and agile force with a strength of about 90,000 personnel. It is involved in war-time and peace-time duties at the border and the surrounding areas. It offers a great career to the officers who wish to be a part of the nations unique and exemplary border guarding force.

National Security Guards(NSG)

The National Security Guards (NSG) is a commando unit originally created for counter-terrorism and hostage rescue missions. Raised in 1986, it is popularly known as the "Black Cats" for the uniform worn by its operators. Like most military and elite security units in India, it is media-shy and the general Indian public is largely unaware of its capabilities and operational details.

The NSG draws its members from the Indian Army and various central police units. It is India's premier counter-terror outfit and is typically deployed in situations that would be beyond the capabilities of regular police units. An NSG team with a dedicated transport aircraft is always stationed at Palam airport in New Delhi, ready to deploy in 30 minutes. The NSG has also been increasingly tasked with protection of VIPs. This role has expanded in recent years, as several politicians have come to view NSG protection as a status symbol. This has caused some concern among senior NSG officers and Home Ministry officials.

Railway Protection Force (RPF)

The Railway Protection Force (RPF) is responsible for law enforcement on Indian Railways. They maintain discipline on platforms as well as travel inside trains to keep passengers secure. Railway accidents are also handled by them.

Special Protection Group (SPG)

The Special Protection Group (SPG) is the executive protection agency of the Government of India. It is responsible for the protection of the Prime Minister of India, other top officials, and their immediate families. The force was established in 1985 after the assassination of Indira Gandhi. It provides the security 24 by 7 all over India to Prime Minister and his Family Members at any location across India. After retirement, the protection & security is provided for the next 10 (Ten) years. Afterwards, it is the responsibility of the respective State Government in which the Prime Minister is residing.

Sashastra Seema Bal (SSB)

The Sashastra Seema Bal, formed in the year 1963, is one of the five main Central Armed Police Forces, deployed at the Indo-Nepal and Indo-Bhutan borders. SSB is an elite and dedicated Central Armed Police Force having more than 82,000 personnel. The SSB personnel are trained in the fields of law & order, military tactics, jungle warfare, counter insurgency and internal security. SSB personnel also serve in the Intelligence Bureau(IB), Research and Analysis Wing (RAW), Special Protection Group(SPG), National Security Guards(NSG) etc. on deputations. The officers start from the level of an Assistant Commandant(A.C), equivalent to the Deputy Superintendent of Police(Dy.SP) in a state and retire at the rank of Inspector General(IG).

Indian Income-tax Department

The Indian Income-tax Department is India's premier financial agency, responsible for a wide variety of financial and fiscal matters.The Tax department is controlled by the Department of Revenue in the Ministry of Finance of the Union Government headed by a Union Minister who reports directly to the Prime Minister.The CBDT is a part of Department of Revenue in the Ministry of Finance. On one hand, CBDT provides essential inputs for policy and planning of direct taxes in India,at the same time it is also responsible for administration of direct tax laws through the Income Tax Department. The Central Board of Direct Taxes is a statutory authority functioning under the Central Board of Revenue Act, 1963. The officials of the Board in their ex-officio capacity also function as a Division of the Ministry dealing with matters relating to levy and collection of direct taxes and matters of tax evasion and revenue intelligence.It is India's official FATF unit. The Income tax Department draws its officers from the Indian Revenue Service officers around the country. It is responsible for investigation into various economic crimes and tax evasion.The special agents and agents are able to carry firearms when they are posted in the Directorate of Criminal Investigation (DCI) in the I-T department.

The DCI is headed by the Director General of Intelligence (Income Tax) which was created to tackle the menace of black money with cross-border ramifications.The revamp is aimed at launching 'un-intrusive' investigations against "persons and transactions suspected to be involved in criminal activities having cross-border, inter-state or international ramifications, that pose a threat to national security and are punishable under the direct tax laws."

The commissioners of the intelligence directorate of I-T who are posted in cities like Delhi, Chandigarh, Jaipur, Ahmedabad, Mumbai, Chennai, Kolkata and Lucknow will also take up criminal investigation work under the DCI. The intelligence wing of the I-T department has the Central Information Branch (CIB) under it, which is a repository of classified and exhaustive data on taxpayers' financial transactions.

Directorate of Revenue Intelligence (DRI)

The Directorate of Revenue Intelligence (DRI) is an intelligence-based organisation responsible for the co-ordination of India's anti-smuggling efforts. Officers in this organisation are drawn from the Indian Revenue Service (I.R.S.).

Narcotics Control Bureau (NCB)

The NCB is responsible for anti-narcotic operations all over the country. It checks the spread of contraband as well as the cultivation of drugs. The officers in this organisation are drawn from IPS and IRS.

Bureau of Police Research & Development (BPR&D)

The Bureau of Police Research and Development (BPR&D) was set up on 28 August 1970 in furtherance of the objective of the Government of India for the modernization of Police Forces. It is involved in a research, relating to problems confronting the Indian police, the training of different ranks of Police in India, and the introduction of technology at both federal and state levels.

National Crime Records Bureau (NCRB)

The National Police Commission in 1979 recommended the creation of a "Nodal Agency" which suggested the maintenance of criminal records at all the police stations in the country and to create shareable databases at police stations and districts and at state and federal Level.

On this recommendation NCRB was created in 1986 with amalgamation of the Directorate of Coordination Police Computers, Central Finger Print Bureau, Data Section of Coordination Division of Central Bureau of Investigation and Statistical Section of the Bureau of Police Research and Development.

Central Forensic Science Laboratory (CFSL)

The Central Forensic Science Laboratory (CFSL) is a wing of the Indian Ministry of Home Affairs, which fulfils the forensic requirements in the country.[1] It houses the only DNA repository in South and Southeast Asia.

There are seven central forensic laboratories in India, at Hyderabad, Kolkata, Mumbai, Rajkot, Chandigarh, Pune and New Delhi. CFSL Hyderabad is centre of excellence in chemical sciences, CFSL Kolkata in biological sciences and CFSL

Chandigarh in physical sciences. These laboratories are under the control of the Directorate of Forensic Science (DFS) of the Ministry of Home Affairs. The laboratory in New Delhi is under the control of the Central Bureau of Investigation (CBI) and investigates cases on its behalf.

National Institute of Criminology and Forensic Sciences (NICFSC)

The National Institute of Criminology and Forensic Science (formerly the "Institute of Criminology and Forensic Science") came into existence on 4 January 1972 on the recommendations of a Committee appointed by the University Grants Commission (UGC) to look into the applied aspects of education, training and research in the fields of Criminology and Forensic Science to commensurate with the growing needs of the country in general and the Criminal Justice System in India in particular. In September 1976, the Institute was constituted as a separate department under the Ministry of Home Affairs headed by a full-time Director.

(C) ACCESS TO JUSTICE

The Indian Judiciary is partly a continuation of the British legal system established by the British in the mid-19th century based on a typical hybrid legal system known as the *Common Law System*, in which customs, precedents and legislative are all components of the law. The Constitution of India is the supreme legal document of the country. There are various levels of judiciary in India – different types of courts, each with varying powers depending on the tier and jurisdiction bestowed upon them. They form a strict hierarchy of importance, in line with the order of the courts in which they sit, with the Supreme Court of India at the top, followed by High Courts of respective states with district judges sitting in District Courts and Magistrates of Second Class and Civil Judge (Junior Division) at the bottom. Courts hear criminal and civil cases, including disputes between individuals and the government. The Indian judiciary is independent of the executive and legislative branches of government according to the Constitution.

The problem of access to justice is deep and pervasive in India and has affected the ability of the legal system and judicial process to respond to injustices. The crisis of delays that has engulfed the Indian judicial process calls for responses at multiple levels of decision-making. A range of reforms — legal, judicial and institutional — needs to be initiated for dealing with delays and ensuring access to justice.

One such important reform is to expand and establish more permanent benches of High Courts in different parts of the country. Historical happenstance has caused the establishment of principal benches of High Courts in different cities in the country. While most States have the principal bench of the High Court located in the capital city, there are a number of States where the principal seat of the High Court is located in another city. Regardless of whether the principal bench of the High Court is in the State capital or not, the imperative of access to justice demands that we move towards establishing adequate benches of High Courts as and when the need arises. The following issues need to be carefully examined while we consider the policy aspects of establishing additional benches of High Courts .

One of the most important lessons of governance in post-Independent India is the recognition that centralisation of power — legislative, executive or judicial — has huge problems in a federal polity. The passing of the 73rd and 74th amendment to the Constitution of India underscored the importance of democratic decentralisation and paved the way for the development of Panchayati Raj institutions. However, the justice delivery mechanisms continue to be centralised and the existing court systems are based on a hierarchical governance structure, which may not be able to effectively address the problems of injustices in the Indian society. The stress that the civil and criminal justice system is facing is also attributed to the lack of capacities of the appellate courts in dealing with disposal of cases.

Establishing more benches of High Courts in more than one city in a State creates new opportunities for people to seek judicial remedies. In fact, the Law Commission of India in its 230th Report dated August 2009 entitled, "Reforms in the Judiciary – Some Suggestions," has persuasively argued for the creation of new benches of High Courts. The report observed: "... It is also necessary that the work of the High Courts is decentralised, that is, more Benches are established in all States ... It is also in the interest of the litigants. The Benches should be so established that a litigant is not required to travel long."

Judicial delays

According to the World Bank, "although India's courts are notoriously inefficient, they at least comprise a functioning independent judiciary". A functioning judiciary is the guarantor of fairness and a powerful weapon against corruption. But people's experiences in fall far short of this ideal. Corruption in the judiciary goes beyond the bribing of judges. Court personnel are paid off to slow down or speed up a trial, or to make a complaint go away. Judges are also subject to pressure from above, with legislators or the executive using their power to influence the judiciary, starting with skewed appointment processes. Citizens are often unaware of their rights, or resigned, after so many negative experiences, to their fate before a corrupt court. Court efficiency is also crucial, as a serious backlog of cases creates opportunities for demanding unscheduled payments to fast-track a case.

Judicial backlog

Indian courts have large backlogs. For instance, the Delhi High Court has a backlog of 466 years according to its chief justice.This is despite the average processing time of 4 minutes and 55 seconds in the court. In Uttam Nakate case, it took two decades to solve a simple employment dispute. However it need to be mentioned that the concept of backlogs doesn't describe the actual reason for so many cases lying in the courts. Rather the term "backlog" has been misused and the term "pendency" is the right word for describing the large number of cases pending in the courts today. As could be understood, the largest numbers of cases that are actually pending in the Indian Courts are that of minor Motor Vehicle Cases, petty crimes such as stealing, abusing, insult, slap, etc. It is an established fact which the Govt. of India accepts that there is 40% shortage of judicial staff. Opposition and ruling party's corrupt politicians profit from the delays in the system.

On 12 January 2012, a Supreme Court bench said that people's faith in judiciary was decreasing at an alarming rate, posing a grave threat to constitutional and democratic governance of the country. It acknowledged some of the serious problems such as –

1. Large number of vacancies in trial courts,
2. Unwillingness of lawyers to become judges,
3. Failure of the apex judiciary in filling vacant HC judges posts.

It wanted to seek answers from the government on amicus :uriae's suggestion that access to justice must be made a :onstitutional right and consequently the executive must provide ıecessary infrastructure for ensuring every citizen enjoyed this ight. It also wanted the Government of India to detail the work ›eing done by the National Mission for Justice Delivery and Legal Reforms.

In October 2012 the BBC reported on the case of Iohammed Idrees, a Pakistani who was held under Indian police ›ntrol for approximately 13 years for overstaying his 15-day visa y 2–3 days after seeing his ill parents in 1999. Much of the 13 :ars was spent in prison waiting for a hearing, and more time as spent homeless or living with generous families. Both states :nied him citizenship, leaving him stateless. The BBC linked ese problems to the political atmosphere caused by the Kashmir ›nflict. There were many similar cases where espionage had been ıarged against non-spies for trivial crimes like overstaying visas minor tresspass, and hundreds of ordinary citizens held in ison by both India and Pakistan. The Indian People's Union for Civil Liberties decried his mistreatment. The Indian Human Rights Law Network told the BBC that the cause was "officials in the home department", including the slow court system, and called the case a "miscarriage of justice, a shocking case".[12]

Judicial corruption

Corruption is rampant in India's courts. According to Transparency International, judicial corruption in India is attributable to factors such as "delays in the disposal of cases, shortage of judges and complex procedures, all of which are exacerbated by a preponderance of new laws".[13] Most disturbing is the fact that corruption has reached the highest judicial forum i.e. Supreme Court of India. Some notable cases include:

1. In December 2009, noted social activist, campaigner for judicial accountability and a Supreme Court lawyer Prashant Bhushan in response to the notice of contempt issued by the Supreme Court (for his interview to a news magazine in which he had said, "out of the last 16 to 17 Chief Justices, half have been corrupt"), filed an affidavit standing by his earlier comments saying: "It is My Honest And Bonafide Perception".Later in September 2010, he submitted a supplementary affidavit in which he submitted evidence to back his allegations.In November 2010, former Law Minister, Shanti Bhushan echoed Prashant Bhushan's claim saying: "It is my firm belief that there is a lot of corruption in judiciary. I am saying the same thing which Prashant Bhushan had said. The question of apology does not arise. I will rather prefer to go to jail. The judiciary cannot be cleansed unless the matter is brought into the public domain".

2. In June 2011, a very widely respected former Chief Justice of India J. S. Verma echoed these views saying that "certain individuals with doubtful integrity were elevated within the higher judiciary" He cited the case of Justice M. M. Punchhi, whose impeachment had been sought by the campaign for judicial accountability. Justice Verma said he was willing to permit the allegations to be probed but the political executive refused to allow this. Justice Verma further explained, "Because the

allegations, if proved, were serious and therefore they required to be investigated, so that one could know whether they were true or not." He acknowledged that Justice Punchhi was later elevated to CJI despite facing "serious allegations". Justice Verma also talked about another former CJI K G Balakrishnan's continuance as National Human Rights Commission chairman. Justice Verma said, "He should have demitted long back and if he doesn't do it voluntarily, the government should persuade him to do that, otherwise, proceed to do whatever can be done to see that he demits office."

3. In November 2011, a former Supreme Court Justice Ruma Pal slammed the higher judiciary for what she called the seven sins. She listed the sins as:

1. Turning a blind eye to the injudicious conduct of a colleague
2. Hypocrisy – the complete distortion of the norm of judicial independence
3. Secrecy – the fact that no aspect of judicial conduct including the appointment of judges to the High and Supreme Court is transparent
4. Plagiarism and prolixity – meaning that very often SC judges lift whole passages from earlier decisions by their predecessors and do not acknowledge this – and use long-winded, verbose language
5. Self Arrogance – wherein the higher judiciary has claimed crass superiority and independence to mask their own indiscipline and transgression of norms and procedures
6. Professional arrogance – whereby judges do not do their homework and arrive at decisions of grave importance ignoring precedent or judicial principle
7. Nepotism – wherein favors are sought and dispensed by some judges for gratification of varying manner.

COSTLY LITIGATIONS

The problem of expensive litigation is one that has been around since the time litigation itself began. The relationship between the cost involved in the process of litigation and the actual worth of the case involved is one that has been subject to scrutiny since time immemorial. In a way, people have grown accustomed to using the word 'expenses' and 'lawsuit' in a synonymous way. Generations of exploitative practices on the part of legal professionals are primarily to be blamed for this attitude of resentment the masses harbour towards the due process of law.

Generally speaking in a broad sense, there are various factors that cause the costs of the price of litigation to go to heights where an average citizen would not even dare to imagine. The factors which are responsible for the increased cost of litigation in our country are both direct and indirect in nature in that certain situations are easier to understand in context of the problem under scrutiny while others require a more precise knowledge of law to ascertain the extent to which it affects the matter at our hands.

Causes of Increasing Costs of Litigation:

1. Prevalence of Legal Ignorance: This is one of the leading reasons why the common man has developed an attitude that borders on utter disgust when it comes to matters of legal proceedings. The average Indian is nowhere near fluent in the matters of general legal knowledge that affects his day to day life. It is the harsh truth that the majority of the population of our country is not completely aware of the concept of the personal rights and liberties that have been guaranteed to them by the Constitution of India. An ignorant person is more likely to be swindled by the many opportunists that our system generates. It is equally deplorable to note here that we mention the general public as being ignorant but all the while we tend to overlook the fact that there exists a large population of advocates that fall well below the standard of an advocate as envisaged by our Constitution framers. At this point in our opening stance it is imperative to address the fact that the issue of ignorance in relation to legal aspects extends from the general populace of our country to the qualified elite who are entrusted with the task of upholding the provisions as laid down in our Constitution. The existence of institutions that award degrees not on the basis of merit but on the sole basis of monetary value is rather disheartening and one might lose hope to learn that the future of the legal system rests partly on such individuals. A sparsely aware advocate might take longer to help his client than an otherwise more aware advocate, and the longer the proceedings for a lawsuit are extended, the longer the client has to incur expenditures.

2. Unnecessary Litigation and Problem of Pendency: Though this is a problem that deserves mention as a different topic altogether, it is nonetheless related to the problem of increasing the costs of litigation. The courts in our country currently face the monumental task of clearing up a colossal amount of cases that have accumulated over the years since we gained our Independence. The figures are shocking to say the least and a number of factors ranging from inadequate infrastructure at the lower levels to acute shortage of judges are the reasons why India has a backlog of almost impossible cases. Once a case gets registered and the proceedings begin, the wheels of the litigation chariot lurch into motion ever so slowly. They carry the weight of only a specified number of cases after which the system grinds to a halt. Only when older cases are decided do the newer cases stand a chance of being resolved and decided. This directly implies that the longer the problem of pendency remains, the more expensive it is for a person to keep pursuing his dream of justice in a court of law.

3. Redundant Formalities and Inefficient system: Another great barrier that comes in the way of a person and the timely justice he deserves is the long list of formalities he has to endure before his case is finally heard in a court. Ranging from small court fees to the attendance required on the part of the litigants, there are a remarkably high number of formalities that a person must observe if he wishes to stand a chance of being heard, let alone provided justice. This is a fact that the Indian Judicial system is known for the efficient and timely manner with which it deals with the winding up of a case, albeit in a negative sense of the word. One fact can firmly be established even when looking from a general perspective that the Indian judicial system is ridden with numerous inefficiencies and endless loopholes that make the issues of speedy justice almost unheard of for a majority of the populace. The client on the other hand is the one who has to bear all the expenses while the proceedings go on. He is the one who is responsible to feed unscrupulous bribes to any official who threatens to impede the process of his attainment of 'justice'. This is again an important point that needs some further looking into. The fact is that the judicial machinery is, as has been stated earlier, suspended in a state of partial immobility and all it takes is a minute omission or petty mistake on the part of the person fighting for justice to bring things to a complete standstill. The system gives refuge to a vast number of people who in the guise of a legal beneficiary can extract money from poor litigants who are none the wiser. For anyone with even basic legal knowledge, it is rather easy to get extensions on court dates and even go so far as manipulate court proceedings. Many cases have been witness to the counsel of either party being involved in unhealthy practices. It is extremely rare for someone to go through the entire machinery of the courts without having to bribe an official or two. The fact that legal professionals in our country are paid rather paltry amounts as remuneration in comparisons to their Western counterparts is also responsible for this behaviour on the part of the officials involved. Insufficient pay scales in accordance with the posts of judges, a dearth of good advocates and the endless opportunities to mislead the client are the reasons why the cost of litigation has artificially gone up. The inefficient structure of the system and the dependence on a multitude of legal formalities means that the time of the trial goes on increasing and that the cost incurred by the person fighting for his right takes a sharp turn in the upward direction.

4. Improper framing of charges: Another practical problem that is responsible for the unnecessary elongation in the duration of the litigation process is the improper framing of charges on the part of the authorities who are responsible for the initial stages of the investigation and legal proceedings. Formative evidence in the early phases of the case history is many a time over looked, manipulated or sometimes completely not paid heed to. Witnesses are not questioned thoroughly or the FIR may be lacking precision in reporting. All these factors are responsible for the incorrect charges to be levelled against either of the two parties. This is related to our problem of increased costs because this can result in two things. Firstly, it may be the reason why a certain someone has been asked to continue on with proceedings for a period longer than would have been otherwise required had the correct charges been levelled. It may also entail the court to penalise someone on the lines of the wrong provisions and that may again lead to increased costs for the already burdened persons involved. This issue is not just for highly technical cases but for rather open and shut cases as well. The prime example is the latest case related to 'suspect' caste killings in the village of Khairlangi. There was enough evidence to invoke the Prevention of Atrocities Act (1989). Four members of a family were publicly humiliated and lynched. They were profusely abused based on their caste and members of the family were hunted down and killed. Two females and two males were the victim of this sadistic act. Neither the Prevention of Atrocities Act nor Sec 354 of the IPC were invoked. The authorities claimed that benefit of doubt be given to the accused for various reasons and the killings were termed as something other than caste related killings. This is to support the point that improper framing of charges is also a prevalent practice that impedes the timely deliverance of justice and quintessentially questions the actual 'cost' of justice.

5. Absence of Settlement Culture & Alternate Dispute Settlement: This particular point is a custom predominantly followed in the western world which has only just begun to emerge in India as a means to reach a mutual understanding without the unnecessary involvement of a court and the usual proceedings that leave both parties in a weaker financial state than when they started and all the more dissatisfied. Alternate Dispute Settlements are most popular in matrimony cases as well as property disputes or other cases relating to family issues where it is possible for the parties to converge and have a healthy discussion that may further lead to a harmonious settlement. ADR's are a less time consuming way of settling disputes for the main reason that they do not involve the usual routine visits to the courts and are easily negotiable. As stated earlier, the time it takes to settle a dispute is directly related to the costs incurred by the parties striving to seek justice. The prevalence of this method might be beneficial in two ways. Firstly, it shall directly reduce the financial burden on the parties involved and helps them to reach a mutually agreed upon compensatory settlement. Secondly, it reduces the burden on the courts and the judiciary thereby not adding to the backlog of already existing cases and thus helping in alleviating a certain amount of stress on the judicial machinery. The relation between the issue of pending cases and increased costs has also been attempted to be clarified earlier.

6. No laws for regulating fees of professionals: It is interesting to note a certain point before we delve deeper into this particular issue. The costs involved in the litigation process are varied. They differ from the court fees to the expense of filing and the cost of the counsel employed by the person seeking justice. The startling fact is that while the court fees and the other charges relating to the proceedings of the court are compulsory and nonnegotiable, they form only a small portion of the actual costs a person has to bear. Mostly it is the fees of the counsel that makes litigition so costly. It is all the more astounding that there exists no law or provision which aims at regulating or capping in any way the fees charged by the lawyer employed by someone. The Indian Advocates Act goes a long way in describing the qualification required for an advocate and also mentions the proper code of conduct. But it does not in any manner put a restriction on the fees charges by the same. The closest provision that prevents the advocate from exploiting the client is the one which states that the advocate shall not be party to any gains monetary or otherwise resulting from the victory of his client. But again, the upper limit is not fixed. The absence of any law or provision to control the fee structure of advocates has been the reason why some advocates charge astronomical amounts. The tragic part is that when it comes to fighting for justice, the common man is helpless and has to seek professional help from registered advocates. Since there are no rules to oblige the advocate to adjust his fee structure in any manner, the unfortunate client has to somehow manage to pay the fees. This is the scene throughout the country where even mediocre and sub-standard advocates have begun indiscriminately exploiting the masses on the pretext of providing justice.

REFERENCES

1. Mishra, O.P. (2006) "Policing in the 21st Century: Areas for Concern", *Indian Police Journal*, Vol. 53, No. 1, (Jan-March), pp. 7-11.
2. Dutta, R.K.(2000) "Policing the New millennium", *Indian Police Journal*, Vol. 47, Nos. 2 & 3, April-Sept 2000, pp. 58-63.
3. Awasthi and Maheshwari "Public Administration" Laxminarayan Aggarwal Publishar. Agra.
4. Bhattacharya, Mohit "New Horizons of Public Administration" Jawahar Publishers.
5. Kashyap, Subhash "Our Political System" (2009) National bank Trust.
6. Sharma, B.K., "Introduction the Constitution of India" (2005) Prentice Hall India.

Web Sources

1. http://www.sunday-guardian.com/investigation/cbi-has-long-history-of-listening-to-its-political-masters-voice
2. http://www.lawteacher.net/terrorism/essays/national-investigation-agency.php#ixzz2vRtlRmS7.
3. http://www.nia.gov.in/mission.aspx
4. http://en.wikipedia.org/wiki/Law_enforcement_in_India
5. http://www.thehindu.com/opinion/lead/expanding-access-to-justice/article5398212.ece.
6. http://www.in.undp.org/content/india/en/home/operations/projects/democratic_governance/access_to_justice/
7. http://doj.gov.in/sites/defau.t/files/userfiles/A2J1.

8. http://indiankanoon.org/doc/506719/

9. http://doj.gov.in/?q=node/107

10. http://lawmin.nic.in/doj/justice/undp/titlepage.htm

11. http://web.worldbank.org/WBSITE/EXTERNAL/COUNTRIES/SOUTHASIAEXT/EXTSAREGTOPPRISECDEV/0,rint:Y~isCURL:Y~content MD:20584873~menuPK:496677~page PK:34004173~piPK:34003707~theSitePK: 496671,00.html.

12. http://www.iimahd.ernet.in/egov/ifip/feb2012/shilpi-varshney.htm.

13. http://www.lawcollegedehradun.com/lawreview/vol.2_issue1_nov10/article5.html

4

RURAL AND URBAN GOVERNANCE: ACCESS TO OPPORTUNITIES AND AMENITIES

NIVEDITA GIRI

Rural Poverty and Migration to Cities: Issues in Access to Food, Employment, Public Health and Education, Impact of Urbanization on Civic Amenities, Infrastructure and Environment

WHAT IS GOVERNANCE ?

Governance according to the Oxford dictionary means a process of collective decision-making and policy implementation. The term is used differently from government. The term refers to reflecting broader concern with norms and a process relating to the delivery of public goods where as government refers to the institutions, rules, and administration of state authority. Government is one of the actors in governance.

The concept of 'governance' is not new. It is as old as human civilization. Governance simply means the process of decision-making and the process by which decisions are implemented or even not implemented. Governance can be used in several contexts such as corporate governance, international governance, national governance, rural governance and urban governance.

The word *governance* derives from the Greek verb '*kubernáo*' which means *to steer* and was used for the first time in a metaphorical sense by Plato[1]. It then passed on to Latin and then on to many languages.

* Assistant Professor, Deptt. of Political Science, Kalindi College, Univ. of Delhi

The general understanding of rural and urban governance is two different regions which are geographically and culturally different from each other. They are known as villages and cities and these areas are interdependent and overlapping. Mismanagement and problems in one area would impact on the other and they are connected due to government structure. In the world there are more rural areas than urban. In the beginning of the 21st century going by the world projection at least 50% constitute rural population and out of that 40% leave in absolute poverty. In India, people in Below Poverty Line (BPL) and Antodaya are living in austerity. Therefore, in search of livelihood rural poor are migrating to urban areas and as a result of that cities are getting crowded.

Rural and Urban Governments are understood as local governments. A local government is an administrative body for a small geographic area, such as a city town, county, or state. A local government will typically only have over their specific geographical region and cannot pass and enforce laws that will affect a wider area. Local government can elect officials, lavy taxes, and do many other things that a national government would do, just on a smaller scale in its own area of jurisdiction. "Local government" only acts within powers delegated to it by legislation or directives of the higher level of government. Each country has some kind of local government which will differ from those of other countries.

RURAL GOVERNANCE

In Indian federation rural local government is understood as Panchayati Raj. It is created in all the States of India by the Acts of concerned State Legislature to establish democracy at the grassroots level. It is based on small units of government, enables people to feel a sense of responsibility and to inculcate the values of democracy. It also gives an opportunity to participate in public affairs, including development work. It is entrusted with the duties and the responsibilities in the field of rural development. Before going detail into it, it would be pertinent to have an understanding of the evolution of local self-government in India.

The Panchayati Raj or the concept of local self government has been the most original and ancient system of local self governance in rural India guaranteeing to people the feel of the direct democracy in modern times.[2] Having a chequered history in evolution and development of the local self government institutions, India stands out as one of the pioneers in taking the reigns of democracy to the very common people in the grassroots level who are considered to the catchments of democracy in any developing country.[3] Routed in the governmental construct of federalism and republicanism as existing in ancient time, the notion of direct democracies in Janapdas and Mahajanapadas, having perspectives seeds of modern days local self government in rural areas, each set to the precursor of Panchayati Raj institutions in the post-independence India. However with the development of city dwelling, the idea of local self government was also expanded to the urban areas, thereby making the notion of local self government two dimensional: rural local self government and urban local self government. While the idea of rural local self government, popularly called the Panchayti Raj seems to be *sui generic* for India owing to its existence in ancient times, the routes of urban local self government are traced back to the British rule in 1687,[4] when a municipal corporation was set up at Madras with a view to transfer the financial burden of local administration to the local city council. Notwithstanding the genesis of urban local self government during the British rule, the colonial ruler proved to be the bane of the local self government particularly the Panchayat Raj, as these institutions fell into utter disregard in the face of the primary concern of the rulers of the day to centralise all the powers in their hands in order to maximise their exploitative gains in India without any hindrance.

In the post-independence times, due to Gandhiji's insistence the idea of Panchayati Raj finding a place in the Constitutional framework of India persuaded the farmers to provide a place of relative insignificance to the dream of Panchayti Raj by placing it in Part IV of the Constitution without any mandatory sanction for the government to operationalise the Panchayti Raj with the inauguration of the Constitution on 26 January 1950.

The Panchayti Raj in India was inaugurated as a consequence of the recommendations of the **Balwant Rai Mehta Committee** (1957) to study the community development programme and national extension service launched in 1952 and 1953 respectively. The Committee submitted its report in November 1957 and recommended the established for the scheme for democratic decentralisation which ultimately came to be known as the Panchayti Raj. The specific recommendations made by it are:[5]

1. Establishment of a three tire system which includes Zilla Parishad at the district level, Panchayt Samiti at the block level, and Gram Panchayat at the village level.
2. These tires should be organically linked together though a device of indirect elections.
3. The village Panchayt should be constituted with directly elected representatives, where as the Panchayt Samiti and Zilla Parishad should be constituted with the indirectly elected members.
4. All the planning and developmental activities should be entrusted to these bodies.
5. The Panchayt Samiti should be the executive body while the Zilla Parishad should be the advisory, and coordinating and supervisory body.
6. The district collector should be the Chairman of the Zilla Parishad.
7. There should be a genuine transfer of power and responsibilities to these democratic bodies.
8. Adequate resources should be transfer to these to enable them to discharge their functions and fulfill their responsibilities.
9. A system should be evolved to effect further devolution of authority in future.

These recommendations were accepted by the National Development Council in January 1958. The Council did not insist on a single rigid pattern and left it to the states to evolve their own patter suitable to the local conditions. But the basic principles and the broad fundamentals should be identical throughout the country. Rajasthan was the first state to establish the institution of Panchayti Raj. The scheme was inaugurated by then Prime Minister Nehru on October 2, 1959, in Nagaur district. Rajasthan was followed by Andhra Pradesh which also adopted the system in 1959. Rajasthan adopted a three tire system. However Tamil Nadu adopted a two tire system and West Bengal adopted a four tire system.

Difficulties in Implementation of Panchayti Raj

Lack of political will -Despite Nehru's initially reluctance he viewed that the three tire system as a model instrument for rural development and during his later time the Panchayti Raj institutions witness the period of ascendancy. He created a new ministry of community development in 1956 and in 1957, the administration of the village Panchayat was transferred to the minister of the community development. Initially the minister for food and agriculture was responsible for coordinating the work of the new ministry with that of his ministry and the new ministry was to work in full cooperation with the ministry of food and agriculture. In 1958, the control of cooperation was also transferred to the ministry of community development and it was renamed as ministry of community development and cooperation. But Nehru's successors did not display same enthusiasm as was shown by Nehru. Lal Bhadur Shastri accepted that "he did not share Nehru's faith in the capacity of the people to rule themselves". Indira Gandhi believed in and established highly centralised polity in which Panchayti Raj Institutions were neglected. She merged the ministry of community development and cooperation with the ministry of food and agriculture.

Centralised tendency -The centralised tendencies in Indian political system were not conducive to a healthy development of Panchayti Raj Institution. The state government also lacked political will to implement Panchayti Raj in its true spirit. They already had a grievance of being assigned less power under the Constitution. They were reluctant in sharing their powers with the Panchayti Raj Institutions. The Bureaucracy also viewed the Panchayti Raj Institutions with utmost content and suspension as a potential threat to its dominating position. The 1970s saw the launching of welfare programmes in rural areas without the Panchayti Raj Institutions being involve in them. For example, pilot research scheme in Growth Centres stated in 1970s and Crash Scheme for rural employment in 1971, Small Farmer's Development Agencies (SFDA) and Marginal Farmer's and Agricultural Labour's Development Agencies (MFAL), Tribal Development Agencies (TDA), Drought Prone Area Programme (DPAP), pilot intensive Rural Employment Project and Agricultural Credit and Marketing were such schemes which created separate agencies outside the sphere of Panchayti Raj Institutions. The subjects assign to PRIs were also taken away, for example village industries which was the responsibility of PRI were assigned to a National Commission as early as in 1953, and these institutions had no role in promoting village industries. Similarly, water supply which was Panchyat's subject was given to new water boards or authorities.

It is also to be remembered that there was a variety of perceptions when the Panchayati Raj was introduced and even after. To the state government, it was an instrument or an agency to implement community development programmes. In some states fears have been expressed that the Panchayati Raj law may undermine regional identities and thus lead to further centralisation at the state level. To politicians particularly at the grassroots level it was a local self government. To people like Jaya Prakash Narayan it was Survodaya, a new social order to replace the existing exploitative system. During Rajiv Gandhi times many felt PRIs were being viewed as the extension of central government's powers at the expense of states government's powers. These different perspectives made the PRIs a political issue and in the process the PRIs suffered. The technology was also a major factor in the decline of Panchayati Raj. After the sever food shortage in 1966-67 the main plank of central government had been to promote new varieties of seeds and other modern concepts to achieve high production. For this purpose Green Revolution was launched under the Central Government's directions. As mentioned above, new schemes were launched which were outside the preview of local self government and eve the state government. The sever food shortage also let to another development detrimental to PRIs. The priorities were reshuffled and there was total emphasis on increasing agricultural production only. "In the process", as S.R. Maheswari says, "a comprehensive concept of rural development got reduced to a mere project for agricultural production."

Lack of adequate of financial resources also hampered the effective functioning of PRIs. The Panchayats could not take up any programme of rural development on their own. They had no access to capital resources. They were entirely dependent upon the central and state government's fund. It was also seen that the Panchayat would become suddenly operational when they received some grants. After the grants were consumed they went back to their slumbers.

Further, the Sarpanch of the Panchayat arrogated all powers of the Panchayat to himself. He had overshadowed the Panchayat as an institution. The other members of the Panchayat hardly took any interest to ensure its smooth functioning. The PRIs also created group rivalries which are the essential consequences of electoral politics and thus vitiated the atmosphere of the villages and hindered the smooth functioning of the system

It is important to mention here that the successive ruling parties of India brought further changes in the PRIs through various committes. In December 1977, the Janata Government appointed **Ashok Mehta Committee** on PRIs. The Commitee submitted its report in August 1978 and made 132 recommendations to revive and strengthen the declining Pranchayati Raj system in the country.

The **GVK Rao Committee** on Administrative Arrangement for the Rural Development and Poverty Alleviation Programmes under the Chairmanship of G.V.K. Rao was appointed by the

Planning Commission in 1985. The Committee came to the conclusion that the developmental process was being gradually bureaucratised and divorced from the Panchayati Raj. The Committee made several recommendation to strengthen and revitalise the Panchayti Raj system.

In 1986, Rajiv Gandhi appointed **L.M. Singhvi Commitee** on the 'revitalisation of the PRIs for democracy and development' under the Chairmanship of L.M. Singhvi. The major recommendations of the Committee are as under:

1. The PRIs should be constitutionally recognised, protected and preserved for this purpose, a new chapter should be added in the Constitution of India. It also suggested some Constitutional provisions to ensure regular, free and fair elections to the Panchayati Raj bodies.
2. Nyaya Pachayat should be established for a cluster of villages.
3. The villages should be organised to make the Gram Panchayat more viable. It also emphasised the importance of the Gram Sabha and called it as the embodiment of district democracy.
4. The village Panchayats should have more financial resources.
5. The judicial tribunals should be established in each state to eradicate controversies about election to the PRIs, their dissolution and other matters related to their functioning.

Constitutionalisation

Besides the above recommendations by various Committees on Panchayati Raj functioning in India, the Narsimha Rao government introduced the Constitutional Amendment Bill in the Lok Sabha in September 1991. It was passed by the Lok Sabha on December 22, 1992 and by the Rajya Sabha on December 23, 1992. Later, it was approved by the 17 State Assemblies and received the assent of the President of India on April 22, 1993. However, the 73rd and 74th Amendment deserves a separate discussion which has been dealt with in the following paragraphs.

73rd and 74th Amendment Act

A giant leap forward was achieved when the 73rd Constitutional Amendment was enacted, which gave Constitutional status to PRIs. In 1993, the political will of the leaders of the day propelled them to design get enacted the 73rd and 74th Constitutional Amendment Acts to lay down some of the landmark provisions regarding the structure, power, and functions of the local self-government at both the rural as well as the urban levels respectively. The 73rd Amendment Act provides for the basic framework of the structure and the functional dynamics of the PRIs and the 74th Amendment Act deals with Municipal government laying down the broad contours of the issues like their structure composition, reservation of seats, elections, powers and functions, finances, and so on.

These two legislations (Acts) created two separate parts in the Constitution, known as Part IX and Part IXA-dealing with the Panchayati Raj and urban local self government respectively. In addition to two new schedules – Schedule Eleventh and Schedule Twelfth, respectively, where the functions of the rural as well as local urban body have been enumerated.

The 73rd Amendment Act 1992 contains Part IX of the Constitution of India. It is entitled as 'The Panchayat' and consist provision of Articles 243, 243-O. the Act has also added the Eleventh Schedule to the constitution of India. It contains 29 functional items of the Panchayats and deals with article 243-G. The Act has given a practical shape to the Article 40 of the Constitution. The Act gives a Constitutional status to the PRIs. The state governments are under the Constitutional obligation to adopt the new Panchayati Raj system in accordance with the provision of the Act. Neither the formation of the Panchayats nor the holding of elections at regular intervals depends on the will of the state governments. The provision of the Act can be grouped into two categories- compulsory and voluntary. The compulsory provisions of the Act to be included in the state laws creating the new Panchayati Raj system. The voluntary provisions, on the other hand may be included in the discretion of the states.

It transfers the representative democracy into the participatory democracy. The salient features of the Act are as follows:

Three tire system

The Act provides for a three tire system of the Panchayati Raj in the states, that is, Panchayat at the village, the intermediate and the district level. The Act defines all the terms in the following manner:

a) Panchayat means an institution (by whatever name called) of local self government for rural areas.

b) Village means, a village specified by the Governor through a public notification to be a village for this purpose and includes a group of villages so specified.

c) Intermediate level means a level between the village and the district specified by the governor trough a public notification for this purpose.

The Act brings about uniformity in the structure of the Panchayati Raj throughout the country. A state having population not exceeding 20 lakh may not constitute Panchayat at the intermediate level.

Important provisions of the Act

Gram Sabha

The Act provides for a Gram Sabha as the foundation of the Panchayati Raj system. Each village with a population of 200 or more has a Gram Sabha. For a cluster of very small villages a common Gram Sabha is created.[6] It is a body consisting of persons registered in the electoral rolls of a village comprised within the area of the Panchayat at the village level. It is a village Assembly consisting of all the registered voters in the area of a Panchayat. It shall exercise such powers and performs such functions at the village level as the state legislature determines.

The main work allocated to the Gram Sabha are; the consideration of the annual statement of accounts, auditing report of the Gram Panchayat, the administrative report of the preceding year, the programme of work for the ensuing year, the taxation proposals and any other specific schemes of a developmental nature involving community service, voluntary labour etc.

Panchayat Act of a state usually provides shall that the Sabha shall at its first meeting considered the budget prepare by the Gram Panchayat and its second meeting consider reports of the working of the Gram Panchayat and draw developments plans for the Sabha area. In Odisha, Palli Sabha can recommended to the Gram Panchayat the development work which should be under taken for execution and also suggests the imposition of enhanced labour-tax on the able-bodied persons living within the Gram Panchayat areas. The Gram Sabha, constitutes the vary base of Panchayati Raj System and as such is a vital institution capable of exerting a big influence on the Gram Panchayat. The Gram Sabha elects the members of the Panchayat and the Chairperson of the Panchayat. It is a real grassroots level institution. The states have now tried to ensure continuance of operation of all the Gram Sabhas in their respective areas.

Gram Panchayat

The Gram Panchayat is the executive organ of the Gram Sabha. It is the most important unit of rural local government. It is directly elected by all the voters living within the area of the Panchayat. There are more than 225000 Gram Panchayats in India.

The membership of the Gram Panchayat varies considerably from 5 to 31. In most of the state Gram Panchayats have 5 to 9 members but in UP from 16 to 31 members. The members of the Panchayat, Panches are elected by all the voters by a secret ballot. In all the states, one-third of seats are reserved for women. Special representation for the Schedule Castes and Schedule Tribes also exist in all the states.

The Sarpanch convenes the meetings of the Panchayat and presides over this. He/She is to convene at least one meeting for month. The Panchs can request him/her for calling a special meeting, which he has to call within three days. He/She keeps the record of the meeting. He/She is responsible for the financial executive function. The Panchayat can assign any function to him/her.[7]

Powers and Functions (Article 243 G)

The State Legislature may endow the Panchayats, with such powers and authority as may be necessary to enable them to function as institution of self government. Such a scheme may contain provision for devolution of powers and responsibilities upon Panchayat at the appropriate level with respect to,

(a) preparation of plans for economic development and social justice;

(b) the implementation of schemes for the economic development and social justice as may be entrusted to them, including those in relation to the 29 matters listed in the Eleventh Schedule.

Gram Panchayat enjoys some power to make general order for the prohibition and regulation of the activities within the Gram Panchayat like use of water of a well, pond, public health etc. it has also power to enquire and report about misconduct of officials within the Gram Panchayat. Gram Panchayat has the power to name the streets and numbering the houses. It performs some judicial functions in respect of some criminal offence within its jurisdiction. Besides this, Gram Panchayat performs some civil revenue and judicial functions. Like suits for the recovery of moveable property or the value of such property etc.

The state government has the power of control over Gram Panchayat. It has the power to remove the Serpanch for abuse of power or misconduct. It can suspend or cancel any resolution of the Panchayat or its functional committees. It has the power to supersede or dissolve the Panchayat. It can suspend or cancel any resolution of the Panchayat or its functional committees.

Panchayat Samiti

The Panchayat Samiti is the intermediate tire in the Panchayati Raj System. In a majority of states, the jurisdiction of a Panchayat Samiti is coextensive with the Block. Panchayat Samiti generally comprises the following categories of members:

a) 6 to 10 members of the Panchayat Samiti are elected directly by the voters of the constituencies falling within the area of the Panchayat Samiti.

b) Elected representative of the Sarpanchs of Panchayats.

c) Local MLAs and MLCs.

d) Persons representing women, SCs and STs whose sets are reserved.

e) In every Panchayat Samiti one-third of the seats are reserved for SCs, STs, women and OBCs.

The term of the Panchayat Samiti is five years. It ordinarily meets at least 6 times each year. A meeting of the Panchayat Samiti is either ordinary or special. The date of every meeting is fixed by the Chairman. The Panchayat Samiti in its very first meeting elects two of its members and Chairman and a Vice-Chairman. The members of a Panchayat Samiti can remove the Chairman by passing resolution by two-third majority.

The duties and functions of the Panchayat are many fold. It does everything necessary to increase agricultural production and other activities relating to it. It looks after animal husbandry and fisheries, health and rural sanitation, social education and many other activities. Its resources mainly consist of a share in the land or local *cess* and duty on transfer of property, community development grant and funds allotted by government or Zilla Parishad. The Panchayat Samiti operates through statutory committees. The Panchayat Samiti like other PRIs have not been very successful in carrying out their work. The team of extension officers led by BDO has however been doing a good work towards the implementation of development schemes.

Zilla Parishad

The Zilla Parishad is the top most tire of the Panchayati

Raj. It operates at the District level and looks after the rural areas of the district. It has the power to acquire, hold and dispose of property and to enter into contracts.

Zilla Parishad has the following categories of members:

- 10 to 25 directly elected members from all the constituencies falling within the area covered by the Zilla Parishad, approximately 50,000 people elect one representative.
- All Chairmen of Panchayat Samities falling within the area of Zilla Parishad.
- MPs and MLAs representing the area.
- Such MPs and MLAs whose names stand registered as voters in any constituency of the area of Zilla Parishad.

Regarding the funds of the Zilla Parishad, all money received by a Zilla Parishad constitutes a fund called the Zilla Parishad fund. Also all money received by the Zilla Parishad is kept in a Government Treasury or Sun-Treasury or in the bank to which the Government Treasury business has been made over. The source of income of a Zilla Parishad consists of the Central and State Governments funds, grants from All India bodies and institutions, state taxes for fees as may be prescribed etc. The expenses of the Zilla Parishad include the salaries and allowances of the officials of the Zilla Parishad, and allowance, if any to be paid to paid to the members of Zilla Parishad or any consultative committee thereof. The Chief Executive officer of a Zilla Parishad in each year frames and places before the Zilla Parishad, on or before the prescribed date, a budget showing the estimated receipt and expenditure during the next financial year.

URBAN GOVERNANCE

There are generally five types of Urban local bodies in India. Since there is no uniformity these bodies varies from city to city. However, Municipal Council enjoys most of the powers and functions in all states. These five types of local bodies are: 1. Corporations, 2. Municipalties, 3. Notified Area Committees, 4. Town Area Committees, and 5. Cantonment Boards.

The first four types are created under state Municipal Laws but the Cantonment Boards are created under the Cantonments Act of 1924. Town Area Committees have now been abolished and converted into Municipal Committees. Town Area Committees are sometimes created for small towns and for small work too. The state Government has the power to propose any area except cantonment as the Nagar Palika.

74th Amendment Act, 1992 deals with the Urban Local Government of India that is Municipality. By this act Part IX A was inserted in the Constitution. After defining the Municipal area and the Municipality, the Amendment Act lays down rules regarding the organisation powers, functions and finances of the institutions of Urban Local Government.

Constitution of Municipalities

A Nagar Panchayat (by whatever name called) for the transitional area, that is to say, an area in transition from a rural area to an urban area;

(a) A Municipal Council for a smaller urban area; and

(b) A municipal corporation for a larger urban area, in accordance with the provision of this part:

Provided that a Municipality under this clause may not be constituted in such an Urban area or part their of as the Governor may, having regard to the size of the area and the Municipal services being provided or proposed to be provided by an industrial establishment in their area and such other factors as he/she may deem fit, by public notification, specify to be an industrial township. All the seats in a Municipality are filled by persons chosen by direct election from the territorial constituencies in the Municipal area and for this purpose each municipal area is divided into territorial constituencies to be known as words. The representation in the Municipality is done in the following manner:

i) Persons having special knowledge or experience in Municipal administration;

ii) The members of the house of the people and the members of the Legislative Assembly of the state representing constituencies which comprise wholly or partly the Municipal area;

iii) The members of the Council of the State and members of the Legislative Council of the state registered as electors with in the Municipal area;

iv) The Chairpersons of the Committees constituted under clause 5 of Article 243S;

Provided that the persons referred to in paragraph (i) shall not have the right to vote in the meetings of the Municipality;

Constitution and Composition of Wards Committees,

There shall be constituted words Committees, consisting of one or more words, with in the territorial area of a Municipality having a population of three lakhs or more. Reservation of seats of Municipality is as same as Panchayat Samiti. 1/3 reservation is given to SCs, STs and women's. Every Municipality, unless sooner dissolved under any law for the time being in force, shall continue for 5 years from the date appointed for its first meeting.

Powers, authority and responsibilities of Municipalities

Subject to the provision of this constitution, the Legislature of the State may, by law, endow –

(a) The Municipalities with such powers and authority as may be necessary to enable them to function as institutions of self-government and such law may contain provision for the devolution of powers and responsibilities upon Municipalities, subject t such conditions as may be specified therein, with respect to –

(i) The preparation of plans for economic development and social justice;

(ii) The performance of functions and the implementations of schemes as may be entrusted to them including those in relation to the matter listed in the Twelfth Schedule;

(b) The Committees with such powers and authority as may be necessary to enable them to carry out the responsibilities conferred upon them including those in relation to the matters listed in the Twelfth Schedule.

Municipalities have the power to impose taxes and also have the power to raise funds.

Every State at the district level a District Planning Committee to consolidate the plans prepared by the Municipalities in the district and to prepare a draft development plan for the district as a whole. In every Metropolitan area a Metropolitan Planning Committee to prepare a draft development plan for the Metropolitan area as a whole. By the 74th Amendment the institutions of Urban Local Government.

RURAL AND URBAN AMENITIES IN INDIA

The state of India through its administration has been engaged in creating, and maintaining amenities and various facilities for the people living in both village and urban areas since its independence. However during British rule there were some amenities available in some areas such as roads, post-offices, schools and health care etc. The rural and urban facilities are taken care of by various departments of both central and state governments. Creating amenities and providing various facilities have been highlighted in the international and national arena since they got included in the Millennium Development Goals. The Goals are ambitious but feasible and, with the support of comprehensive United Nations development agenda, the government efforts are on to achieve these by 2015. In the recent years, many international agencies like UNDP, UNESCAP, UN-HABITAT, Asian Development Bank (ADB), World Bank and others have advocated and highlighted the importance of basic amenities for well-being and raising the standards of living. They have also laid down initiatives, assistance, norms and standards.

Rural Amenities

India's economic growth and development is predicated to a large extent upon the development of its 700-million strong rural population. Majority of the population lives in about

600,000 small villages and are engaged primarily in agriculture, directly or indirectly. A substantial portion of India's current agricultural labor force has to move to non-agriculture sectors for income. The challenge is to manage the transition of 80% of the rural population from a village-centric agricultural-based economy to an industry based economy.

The Government has launched **"Bharat Nirman"** programmes for the development of rural infrastructure. Access to basic amenities like drinking water, sanitation, electricity, housing, drainage and others are crucial to the well-being as they contribute to physical and material comfort and quality of life. They also benefits by ensuring better health, environment and providing opportunities for other useful activities.

There are centrally sponsored schemes for rural development and poverty eradication such as NREP, TRYSEM, IRDP etc. have not been much of a success. The lack of success is not due to faulty premises underlying the schemes but the fact that absence of people's involvement in the formulation, implementation and evaluation of these schemes to a needed extent. These programmes have been in a way imposed on rural people without understanding their requirements. The suitability of a scheme in a particular area has also been overlooked. The emphasis has been on completing targets rather than actually helping people. To give an example, TRYSEM (Training Rural Youth for Self Employment) has been introduced in areas where people are more inclined towards wage employment. No development programme can achieve its targets if it does not keep in view the needs of the people, and all those affected. Development programmes must also try to satisfy the basic needs of people such as food. shelter, clothing and health.

There have been several initiatives, plans and programmes in India to improve the access to basic amenities. Since, rural and urban areas have different set of administrative arrangements and needs, separate plans and programmes are designed for them. For the development of India's rural areas, the Bharat Nirman (2005) was launched. Under Bharat Nirman, action is proposed in the areas of irrigation, road (Pradhan Mantri Gram Sadak Yojana), rural housing (Indira Awaas Yojana), rural water supply, rural electrification (Rajiv Gandhi Grameen Vidyutikaran Yojana) and rural telecommunication connectivity. There are also programmes of Ministry of Rural Development, such as Rajiv Gandhi National Rural Drinking Water Programme, Total Sanitation Campaign (which is renamed as Nirmal Bharat Abhiyan in May 2012) and others. Another landmark initiative came in 2004 with the launch of Provision of Urban Amenities to Rural Areas (PURA). PURA is a strategy for rural development in India; the primary objectives of the scheme are the provision of livelihood opportunities and urban amenities in rural areas to bridge the rural-urban divide. Besides, there are other programmes for rural people like Nirmal Gram Puraskar (NGP), Rural Habitations with Adequate Safe Drinking Water Supply under National Drinking Water Program (NRDWP), and Nearest Education and Health Related Facility.

MAHATMA GANDHI NATIONAL RURAL EMPLOYMENT GURANTEE ACT (MGNREGA)

The Mahatma Gandhi National Rural Employment Guarantee Act (MGNREGA) is the law that aims to guarantee the 'right to work' and ensure livelihood security in rural areas by providing at least 100 days of guaranteed wage employment in a financial year to every household whose adult members volunteer to do unskilled manual work.[8] The statute is hailed by the government as "the largest and most ambitious social security and public works programme in the world".[9]

Targeting poverty through employment generation using rural works has had a long history in India that began in the 1960s. Unlike earlier rural development programmes, MGNREGA guaranteed employment as a legal right. However, the problem areas are still the same as they were in the 1960s. The most significant ones are- lack of public awareness, mismanagement and above all mass corruption. The more comprehensive survey of Comptroller and Auditor General (CAG) of India, a 'Supreme Audit Institution' defined in Article

148 of the Constitution of India, reports serious lapses in implementation of the act.[10] The CAG also suggests a list of recommendations to the government for corrective measures.

At minimum wage rate and within 5 km radius of the village, the employment under MGNREGA is an entitlement that creates an obligation on the government failing which an unemployment allowance is to be paid within 15 days. Along with community participation, the MGNREGA is to be implemented mainly by the Gram Panchayats (GPs). The involvement of contractors is banned. Labour-intensive tasks like creating infrastructure for water harvesting, drought relief and flood control are preferred. Another objective of the Act is to generate productive assets, protecting the environment, empowering rural women, reducing rural-urban migration and fostering social equity, among others."

For effective management, the legislation also mentions implementation principles and key agencies. The principles are: collaborative partnership and public accountability; community participation; Panchayats as principal authorities; overall responsibility of district programme coordinator (DPC) and programme officer (PO); coordination among agencies; and resource support. The agencies are: Gram Sabha and Gram Panchayat at the village level; intermediate Panchayat and PO at the block level; district Panchayats and DPC at the district level; State Employment Guarantee Council (SEGC), state government and employment guarantee commissioner at the state level; and central employment guarantee council (CEGC) and Ministry of Rural Development at the central level.

The Prestigious MGNREGA scheme proposed providing livelihood and urban amenities in compact areas around a potential growth centre in Gram Panchayats through Public Private Partnership (PPP) framework to provide guarantee employment to rural areas so that they could have an assured income for at least 100 days of a year. The scheme is now facing rampant corruption, cases of underpayment of wages have been received by the government from all over the country.

RURAL POVERTY AND MIGRATION TO CITIES

Poverty has social, economic and political dimensions. It refers to the condition of not having the means to afford basic human needs like clean water, nutrition, health care, education, clothing, shelter and lack of economic opportunities that provides commensurable income to access 'basic needs'. It also refers to lack of opportunities to participate in decision making that affect their social and economic life. Poverty in India is defined based on calorie norm of 2,400 per capita per day for rural areas and 2,100 per capita per day for urban areas.[7] The poverty line for the base year 1973-74 was taken as the per capita expenditure level, which meets these calorie norms on an average, for the country as a whole, as per the National Sample Survey (NSS) household consumption expenditure survey for the corresponding year. In order to arrive at the estimates of the number of poor, Planning Commission has been making adjustments in the NSS data on distribution of households by consumption expenditure levels. Based on this methodology, estimates of poverty – both urban and rural – are being made at national and state levels by the Planning Commission at five-year intervals since 1973. The poverty line at all-India level is worked out from the expenditure per capita per month class-wise distribution of persons (based on URP-consumption, that is, consumption data collected from 30 –day recall period for all items) and the poverty ratio at all-India level. The poverty ratio at all-India is obtained as the weighted average of the state-wise poverty ratio. Similar exercise is carried out for the states also. In 2001, for the first time, Census also captured the slum demography details, though the data was collected only from class I and II cities of 1991 Census. States have also been conducting poverty surveys in urban local bodies as part of SJSRY and other programs for better targeting the poverty programs.

Poverty has both economic and social dimensions; though only income aspects have always been highlighted. Lack of access to basic services like water, sanitation, health, educations, housing, etc., are signifies levels of poverty. Therefore, the Planning

Commission periodically identifies the poverty line state-wise which becomes the basis for calculating the state level poverty and fund allocation.

Lack of livelihood opportunities, modern amenities and services for decent living in rural areas results in a sense of deprivation and dissatisfaction amongst a large percentage of population and leads to migration of people to urban areas. This is primarily due to the wide gaps in the availability of physical and social infrastructure between rural and urban areas. In order to address these issues, the Government, in the past has launched various schemes at different points of time. However, due to several reasons the impact has not been very visible. The deliveries of these schemes were not simultaneous and although huge sums were earmarked for capital expenditure, very little resources were spent on the operation and maintenance of the assets. Also, each of these schemes operated autonomously and the standards set for infrastructure services delivery in the rural areas was far below those for the urban population. Hence, in spite of several schemes, there continued to be a substantial flow of migration from the rural to urban areas. In order to catalyze the convergence between different infrastructure schemes and create a new model for management of urban services in the rural areas, the Provision for Urban Amenities in Rural Areas (PURA) scheme has been developed.

After India gained its independence, despite of a plethora of welfare schemes and activities aimed at rural areas in successive five year plans, there remained huge development gaps between urban and rural areas. Lack of livelihood opportunities, modern amenities and services for decent living in rural areas lead to migration of people to urban areas. There are wide gaps in the availability of physical and social infrastructure between rural and urban areas. To address these issues, on the eve of India's 54 Republic Day in 2003, the President of India A.P.J. Abdul Kalam highlighted a vision of transformation of rural India by launching a large-scale mission for Provision of Urban Amenities in Rural Areas (PURA)[11].

PURA Scheme

PURA was envisaged as a self-sustainable and viable model of service delivery to be managed through an implementation framework between the different stakeholders involved local people, public authorities and the private sector. The Government support would be in the form of finding the right type of management structure to develop and maintain rural infrastructure, empowering the management structure and providing initial economic support.

The mission of the PURA scheme is holistic and accelerated development of compact areas around a potential growth centre in a Gram Panchayat (or cluster of contiguous Gram Panchayats) through Public Private Partnership (PPP) framework for providing urban amenities and livelihood opportunities to improve the quality of life in rural areas. The scheme aims to provide urban amenities and livelihood opportunities in rural areas to bridge the rural-urban divide. Core funding shall be sourced from the convergence of Central Government schemes and complemented by additional support through the PURA scheme. The private sector shall also bring on board its share of investment besides operational expertise. The PURA scheme would be implemented and managed by the private sector on considerations of economic viability but designed in a manner whereby it is fully aligned with the overall objective of rural development.

PURA proposes that urban infrastructure and services be provided in rural hubs to create economic opportunities outside of cities. Physical connectivity by providing roads, electronic connectivity by providing communication network, and knowledge connectivity by establishing professional and Technical institutions will have to be done in an integrated way so that economic connectivity will start. The Indian central government has been running pilot PURA programs in several states since 2004.

The agriculture in India has been growing just at 1.6%. To uplift the two hundred and twenty million people living below poverty line and provide improved quality of life, the government has to ensure that the agricultural sector grows at least at 4% per annum. For providing this growth, there need to spread the development process to the rural sector. That is what the PURA programme involving four connectivity, namely physical, electronic and knowledge leading to economic connectivity, envisages. Hence, the entire country should have 7,000 PURAs encompassing over 600,000 villages. The theme of PURA, apart from concentrating on reinforcing agriculture, will emphasise on agro-processing, development of rural craftsmanship, dairy, fishing, and silk production, so that the non-farm revenue for the rural sector is enhanced, based on the core competence of the region. Also the rural economy will be driven by renewable energy such as solar, wind, bio-fuel and conversion of municipal waste into power. In this approach, the aim is to make sustainable development using the core competence of the rural sector. Government, private and public sectors have been taking up rural development in parts. For example, setting up educational institutions and healthcare centres, laying roads, building houses, building a marketing complex, giving a communication link in a particular rural area have been taken up in the past as individual activities. For the first time, PURA envisages an integrated development plan with employment generation as the focus, driven by provision of the habitat, healthcare, education, skill development, physical and electronic connectivity and marketing.

The PURA scheme is implemented by District Rural Development Agencies (DRDAS), Ministry of Rural Development, Government of India. In **process for implementation of the PURA scheme,** a Gram Panchayat/a cluster of geographically contiguous Gram Panchayats for a population of about 25,000 to 40,000 is identified.

A list of infrastructure, urban amenities and economic activities to be provided under PURA are:

- Water and sewerage
- Village streets

- Drainage
- Solid waste management
- Skill development
- Development of economic activities
- Solar village street lighting
- Telecom
- Non conventional electricity generation
- Village linked tourism
- Integrated Rural Hub, Rural Market
- Agri–common service centre and warehousing
- Any other rural economy based project

At least one such activity would be included in the PURA project. An activity from the list of Add-on Economic projects could be included in the activities. Hence, amenities under Ministry of Rural Development (MoRD) Schemes includes that the Concessionaire shall be responsible for delivering amenities and services such as water and sewerage, construction and maintenance of village streets, drainage, solid waste management and skill development under the following ongoing schemes of the MoRD such as Special Projects for Skill Development of Rural Youths under Swarnjayanti Gram Swarozgar Yojana (SGSY), National Rural Drinking Water Programme (NRDWP), Total Sanitation Campaign (TSC), etc. For development of economic activities, support may also be drawn from the National Rural Livelihood Mission (Restructured SGSY).

The PURA may include schemes of other central government ministries and state government ministries, that are available "on tap" as some areas of critical infrastructure (urban amenities) necessary for the project are not within the purview of the MoRD, such as Ministry of Panchayati Raj (Rural Business Hub scheme and others), Ministry of New and Renewable Energy (for solar village street lighting and non conventional electricity generation) and Ministry of

Communications and Information Technology (for telecom services) etc. The Concessionaire shall access the support under such schemes of relevant Ministries other than MoRD and dovetail into PURA for delivering the identified urban amenities.

On the basis of the terrain and climatic conditions there could be four types of PURA in the country - Plain terrain PURA, Hill PURA, Coastal PURA, and Desert PURA. The population in the plain terrain and coastal region PURA may be in the region of 20,000 to 100,000 in a cluster of 20 to 30 villages, whereas in the Hill or desert PURA may have a population of 7,500 to 15,000 people in a cluster of 30 to 50 villages or hamlets.

Seven pilot projects were implemented during the 10th Five Year Plan in Basmath (Maharashtra), Bharthana (Uttar Pradesh), Gohpur (Assam), Kujanga (Orissa), Motipur (Bihar), Rayadurg (Andhra Pradesh) and Shahpura (Rajasthan). An evaluation study of these pilot projects was carried out by (NIRD) National Institute of Rural Development which identified the necessity of community and private sector participation as essential factors and the need for factoring infrastructure development with lead economic activities and livelihoods creation, requirement of project site selection on the basis of growth potential and need for convergence with other schemes of the government. Based on the findings of the evaluation study by NIRD, comments, feedback received from different stakeholders like various Ministries/ Departments, feedback received during consultations with private sector representatives and officials of State Governments, and the recommendations of the consulting team of Asian Development Bank), the scheme of PURA has been restructured for implementation on pilot basis during 11th Five Year Plan as a Central Sector scheme. Through the implementation of proposed pilot projects at different places of India different from each other, the unique features of this scheme would be tested on the ground that will provide lessons for upscaling in the future and extending PURA throughout the country.Besides, the entire process shall help strengthen the institutional ability of a Gram Panchayat to undertake PPP and help pilot-test the viability of PPPs in rural infrastructure development.

Thrust Areas for PURA

Thrust areas for PURA would be the following:

- Creation of employment opportunities for all the employable people, particularly the youth.
- Capacity building in education - school, value-added employable skills and knowledge.
- Provision of quality health and timely healthcare, safe drinking water, quality-reliable electric power, energy-efficient and water-efficient pucca houses.
- Typical examples of PURA connectivities - physical, electronic, knowledge and economic - to be included in the PURA project

PURA has taken as a business proposition of Rs. 100 crores with public and private partnership over a project period of five years. Government (Bharat Nirman Programme, Rural Development Ministry, Prime Minister Sadak Yojana, Prime Minister Rozgar Yojana, Sampoorna Graha Yojana, Navodaya Schooling, 100 days Employment Guarantee Scheme and State Government Employment programmes); banks (National Bank for Agriculture and Rural Development, Asian Development Bank, World Bank, United Nations Development Programme, United Nations Children's Fund, United Nations Educational, Scientific and Cultural Organisation (UNESCO) and venture capitalists can fund PURA components. Some states such as Chhattisgarh, Karnataka and Kerala have taken up the PURA as a programme for implementation because government initiatives and also certain private initiatives have established working PURAs in Tamilnadu, Maharashtra, Madhya Pradesh and Andhra Pradesh.

PURA projects are functioning in different parts of the country. Some of them are Periyar PURA, Loni PURA, and Byrraju PURA. Periyar PURA complex pioneered by Periyar Maniammai College of Technology for Women, Vallam, Tanjore is functioning near Vallam with a cluster of over 65 villages in Tamilnadu, which involves a population of one lakh. This PURA complex has all the three connectivities - physical, electronic and knowledge - leading to economic connectivity. Periyar PURA has healthcare centres, primary to postgraduate-level education and vocational training centres. This has resulted in large-scale employment generation and creation of number of entrepreneurs with the active support of 850 self-help groups. Two hundred acres of waste land has been developed into a cultivable land with innovative water-management schemes such as contour ponds and water sheds for storing and irrigating the fields. All the villagers are engaged in cultivation, planting Jatropha, herbal and medicinal plants; power generation using bio-mass; food processing and above all running marketing centre. This model has emanated independent of any government initiative. The committed leadership has been provided by the engineering institution. Recently, five of the Periyar PURA villages are connected through WiMAX wireless and have minimum 4 megabits per second connectivity with the Periyar PURA nodal centre. It provides a sustainable economic development in that region.

Loni PURA in Maharashtra where a participative model of integrated rural development has come up amongst 44 villages with a population of 80 thousand. The Loni PURA model has been pioneered by Pravara medical trust. It is improving the productivity of the rural people through improved quality of life with healthcare, education and employment. The concept is people-centric development for social transformation. The thrust area of development has been on comprehensive medicare, particularly for women and children, need-based health education and e-connectivity to the farmers. The complex has created 27 educational and vocational institutions consisting of schools, colleges, polytechnic and industrial training institutes (ITIs) including medical and engineering colleges. They have created a sugar factory, bio-gas plants, chemical plants and power projects. They have a large number of self-help groups for providing low-interest loan for the weaker sections of the society. Because of the co-operative effort of the people, literacy in these villages has gone up from 63 to 83%, birth rate has come down, infant mortality has decreased to 35/1,000 from 70/1,000 and the standard of living of the people has gone up by over 20% compared with other villages in the neighbouring areas.

In Andhra Pradesh, Byrraju Foundation of Satyam near Bhimavaram has undertaken the mission of establishing 32 Ashwini centres, benefiting 116 villages with a population of around 500,000 people. It has provided the electronic connectivity through wireless (512 kilobits per second – 2 megabits per second) and knowledge connectivity in co-operation with National Academy of Construction, Hyderabad and other domain experts, thereby creating economic connectivity in these villages. During the last few years of its operation, it has skill-enabled and knowledge enabled-people in areas such as construction, tailoring, garment production, Information technology (IT) and spoken English skills. This programme resulted in 3,000 jobs with the minimum earning of Rs. 3,000 per month, which is three times that of their earlier earning potential. A rural business process outsourcing (BPO) Gram IT, established in Jallikakinada centre, has trained the unemployed graduates in IT skills and spoken English and employed 100 people for the BPO operations such as transaction processing of Human Resource data of Satyam Computers as a back office processing; data processing of 1 million self-help-group members of Andhra Pradesh such as financial data, accounting data, spending pattern, cultural aspects under the programme of 'Mapping the bottom of the Pyramid'. This Gram IT BPO has affected the 10% reverse migration from Hyderabad to Bhimavaram. This model can be replicated by many of our IT companies in the rural sector to create PURA clusters and bring rural transformation.

OUTCOMES OF PURA

This PURA complex would have transformed into a dynamic rural complex with focus on employment potential for all the families of PURA cluster with all the connectivities. This PURA complex will have its umbilical connectivity with the nearest university. However, PURA we have discussed:

- Provide to all the village citizens dwelling units with clean water supply and sanitation facilities.
- The village complex will have 100% literacy.
- Apart from upgrading existing schools, the complex will have a few colleges; world-class vocational training institutions in construction, carpentry, welding, and natural art; computer maintenance and services; IT-enabled services; BPO and a call centre. The 'Sakshat' programme a one-stop education portal, will be used through Internet for capacity building in this region,
- People in the PURA complex will be able to get quality healthcare through telemedicine and mobile clinics via primary health centres. They will be brought under a corporate medical healthcare scheme.
- Each PURA village complex will be free from diseases such as polio, TB, leprosy and malaria and other waterborne diseases. The infant mortality will be less than 10.
- The PURA complex will promote horticulture and floriculture products, apart from agriculture in collaboration with nearby agricultural universities and research institutions.
- There will be agro-processing industries in each PURA complex for value addition to horticulture produce.
- Creation of dairy and fish farms in each PURA complex for providing additional non-farm revenue to farmers. They can also produce other dairy products.
- Revival of all existing water bodies in the PURA cluster.
- Provision of employment to all employable people of the village through additional jobs in dairy, agro-processing, construction, handicraft and tourism enterprises.
- Overall, per capita income of the PURA cluster should increase three times and people living below the poverty line should come down to zero in 6 years.

Failure of PURA

Rural Development Minister Jairam Ramesh on 24 February 2012 launched the restructured PURA scheme that combines rural infrastructure development with economic regeneration in Private Public Partnership (PPP) mode and seeks to harness the efficiencies of the private sector. He slammed former president APJAbdul Kalam's concept of PURA(Providing Urban Amenities in Rural Areas) as a failure. Ramesh said that while the PURA Launched by Kalam has failed, the reworked PURA will succeed. The minister was optimistic about the success of the new PURA because of the difference in the objectives. He was of the view that, now the focus was on water supply, sanitation, physical infrastructure rather than knowledge connectivity.

The Rural ministry plans to reform one of its ambitious yet not so successful programme – Provision of Urban amenities in Rural Areas (PURA) – to facilitate creation of urban infrastructure in around 2,000 new towns that have been identified by the 2011 decadal Census. It is also trying to restructure the old PURA objectives as well.

URBAN AMENITIES

In order to usher in an era of urban governance the Eleventh Plan reaffirmed the vitality of the Jawaharlal Nehru Urban Renewal Mission (JNNURM) that was launched by the Government of India in December 2005. The Mission aims at improving and augmenting the economic and social infrastructure of 65 select cities as well as affordable housing and basic services to the urban poor through planned development of the identified cities, calling for the strict implementation of the Seventy Fourth Amendment Act, Urban Local Bodies.[12]

The JNNURM is expected to cater to the non-mission towns and cities under the two components, namely, the Urban Infrastructure Development Scheme for Small and Medium Towns (UIDSSMT) and the Integrated Housing and Slum Developmer Programme (IHSDP). The programme is expected to cover all other census towns under the UIDSSMT. The existing programme of Infrastructure Development Scheme for Small and Medium Towns (IDSMT) and Accelerated Urban Water Supply Programme (AUWSP) has been subsumed under UIDSSMT. Like-wise, the existing Valmiki Ambedkar Awas Yojana (VAMBAY) and the discontinued National Slum Development Programme (NSDP) have been subsumed in the IHSDP. Another programme dovetailed with the JNNURM is the Interest Subsidy Scheme for Housing Urban Poor (ISHUP) aims to provide a stimulus to housing programmes under the public-private partnership mode.

Urban Poverty

Over decades the urban poverty has been increasing whereas the rural poverty has been declining. Among the total poor in the country, the per centage of rural poor was 83.77 in 1973-74 while it came down to 73 % by 2004-05. But in case of urban poverty there has been an increase in the levels of poverty. In 1973-74 the per centage of urban poor to total poor was only 16% where as in 2004-05 it has increased to 27%, signifying increase in urban poverty in the country. In some states it is more prominent. For example, in the southern states of Andhra Pradesh, Karnataka and Kerala and northern states of Rajasthan and Delhi the urban poverty is far higher than rural poverty.

Urban slums are physically and socially deteriorated residential areas where it is difficult to live. Bad housing, inadequate light and air, absence of sanitation facilities overcrowding, absence of recreational facilities, vulnerability to fire and other natural disasters, etc., characterize the slums. For purposes of census, the Registrar General of India considers all those recognized as slums by the state Slum Acts, Housing and Slum Boards – notified or non-notified, and those areas with at least 300 people or 60-70 households, tenements with unhygienic environment, inadequate infrastructure and absence of proper water, sanitation, etc. The slum population is constantly increasing; it has doubled in the past two decades. The current population living in slums in the country is more than the population of Britain. A survey in 2002 identified 51,688 slums in urban areas of which 50.6% were declared as "notified slums." The growing slum population and the lack of basic facilities will badly impact on India's overall target achievement in water and sanitation sector.

Poverty, as noted earlier, relate to inadequacy of income, poor access to basic amenities, and lack of voice in public affairs. It is with regard to the latter two slums manifest a form of poverty. Absence of tenurial security, constant fear of eviction, vulnerability to disasters, insecure employment, over-crowding and unhealthy living environment, etc., are some of the factors that make slums some of the worst manifestations of urban poverty. There is no authentic data on slum population either at city or state levels. Except Census 2001 and 2011data on slum population was never collected by official agencies any time in the past. As a result planning for their development and fund allocation has always been ad hoc.

Infant mortality rate (IMR) explains the health status of the community. The urban infant mortality rate has been declining over years in the states. But there are wide variations between states. The national average in 2008 is 36. In Kerala it is as low as 10 while in states like UP and Orissa it is as high as 49.[14] About 2.3% do not have exclusive room in their house, 35% have one room and 29.5% have two rooms. Total housing shortage in the country was estimated at 24.7 million houses of which shortage for Economically Weaker Section category is 21.78 millions and for Lower Income Group category 2.89 million and the rest is for the other categories. Recognising the importance of affordable housing to the poor to improve their living conditions and quality of life under BSUP and IHSDP over 15.4 lakh houses were sanctioned by the Ministry of Housing and Urban Poverty Alleviation. Of them 8.22 lakh houses were completed or nearing completion which is a significant achievement.

Policies and Programmes

The Government of India has been giving focus to urban development and poverty aspects right from the First Five Year Plan. In the first three five year plans focus was on housing upgradation and slum clearance programs. During fourth and seventh plans the focus was on urban community development and environmental improvement of slums. From eighth plan on words urban poverty began to get attention and a series of programs relating to basic services and livelihoods and employment generation were launched. The evolution of urban development and poverty reduction policies and programs is given as under:

First Plan-(1952-56) - Housing Development.

Second Plan- (1956-61) - Urban community development started in 1958. Housing, Slum clearance and improvement, Land development

Third Plan - (1961-66) - Housing programs for low income groups; Loans to State Governments to acquire land to make available building sites

Fourth Plan - (1969-74) - Expansion of urban community development; Establishment of Housing and Urban Development Finance Corporation to fund housing and urban development programs, especially to the poor; Launching of Environmental Improvement of Urban Slums (EIUS) to provide minimum level of services to poor

Fifth Plan-(1974-79) - Enactmet of Urban Land (Ceiling and Regulation) Act to make available land for construction of houses for the middle and low income groups; EIUS was transferred as a state scheme in 1974

Sixth Plan-(1980-85) - Urban Basic Services (UBS) program was started in 1981 to cater to the basic physical and social needs of the poor

Seventh Plan- (1985-90) - First conscious effort to directly address problem of urban poverty; UBS program extended to 168 towns in partnership with UNICEF; Adoption of four-pronged strategy to address urban poverty viz., employment generation through micro-enterprises and public works, housing and shelter upgradation, social development with focus on women and children, environmental upgradation of slums; Launching of Nehru Rozgar Yojana (NRY) in 1989 and UBSP in 1990

1990-92 - Enactment of Constitution 74th Amendment Act, 1992; Urban poverty alleviation, slum upgradation and protection of interests of weaker sections as legitimate function of ULBs (as part of 12th Schedule of the Constitution)

Eighth Plan-(1992-97) -Launching of Prime Minister's Integrated Urban Poverty Eradication Program (PMIUPEP) in 1995 for Class II towns; Launching of National Slum Development Program in 1996

Ninth Plan-(1997-2002) - Launching of Swarna Jayanti Shahari Rojgar Yojana in 1997 by subsuming NRY, PMIUPEP and UBSP; Launching of Valmiki Ambedkar Awas Yojana (VAMBAY) to provide or upgrade shelter to slum dwellers. National City Sanitation Project called Nirmal Bharat Abhiyan was an integral part of VAMBAY

Tenth Plan-(2002-07)

- Launching of Jawaharlal Nehru National Urban Renewal Mission (JnNURM) in 2005 for the identified 65 Mission cities;
- Basic Services to the Urban Poor is an integral component of JnNURM;
- Integrated Housing and Slum Development Program (IHSDP) was launched for the non-mission cities.

Eleventh Plan-(2007-12)

- Creating and updating database on slums;
- Granting tenure security and provision of affordable housing; Provision of land for the poor in the master plans;
- Developing self-employment enterprises and job creation;
- Protection of economic interest & safety of women and vulnerable sections;
- City-wise perspective and integrated slum development plans;
- Augmenting and facilitating access to services for slum dwellers;

- In-situ upgradation and resettlement options for slum improvement;
- Using land as a resource for shelter development for slum dwellers

Urban poverty alleviation is one of the important objectives of five-year plans. As it is a multi-dimensional, innovative and coordinated actions are needed at macro and micro levels. Several programs and schemes sponsored by both central and state governments are in operation. They aim to strengthen and improve the quality and standard of living of weaker and deprived sections of the society. Different government departments/ corporations of state governments constantly make efforts to eradicate poverty and to generate sources for raising income and employment in the state. Though the incidence of poverty has come down over decades, the number of poor in the country has remained more or less stable due to rise in population.

A number of urban development and urban poverty alleviation programmes are under implementation in states. Some of these programmes are sponsored by the Government of India and others launched by the State Governments. The programs launched by the Government of India include:

a) Urban community development program (1958)
b) Subsidised housing program (1970)
c) Environmental Improvement of Urban Slums and Low Cost Sanitation Program (1972)
d) Slum Improvement Programs (1983- externally aided)
e) Urban Basic Services (1985)
f) Nehru Rozgar Yojana (1989)
g) Urban basic services for the poor (1991)
h) Prime Ministers Integrated Urban Poverty Alleviation Program (1995)
i) National Slum Development Program (1996)
j) Swarna Jayanti Shahari Rozgar Yojana (1998, Revamped in 2009)

k) Valmiki Ambedkar Awas Yojana (2001)
l) National Policy for Urban Street Vendors (2004)
m) Basic Services for the Urban Poor (*Jn*NURM, 2005)
n) Integrated Housing and Slum Development Program (2005)
o) Interest Subsidy Scheme for Housing the Urban Poor (ISHUP) – 2008
p) Integrated Low Cost Sanitation (ILCS Revamped in 2008)
q) Urban Statistics for HR & Assessments (USHA) – 2008
r) Affordable Housing in Partnership Scheme – 2009
s) National Policy on Urban Street Vendors – 2009
t) Slum-free City Planning Scheme for Rajiv Awas Yojana – 2010

Each of the schemes has a specific focus, objectives and components. For example, UCD focused on participation and self-help programs. The SJSRY aims at motivating the under employed and unemployed - both individuals and groups - to start micro-enterprises. There is also provision for wage employment. This Yojana rests on the foundations of community empowerment and local bodies' works through community based organizations in implementing the programme. The components of the programme include Self-employment through micro-enterprises, Development of Women and Children in urban areas and Entrepreneurship and vocational skill development of urban poor. An analysis of the implementation of poverty alleviation policies and programmes brings out the following important features:

- Fragmented approach to urban poverty by individual departments, schemes and programmes,
- Lack of convergence and integration,
- Lower priority to urban as compared to rural –education and health,
- Limited focus on slum development – tenure, services etc.,
- No separate funding for urban poverty/poor,
- Missing linkages across departments, sectors and funds,

Finance Commission. The focus is on making urban local bodies (ULBs) accountable for efficient management of cities.

END NOTES

1. http://ec.europa.eu/governance/docs/doc5_fr.pdf
2. Bidyut Chakravarty and R.K. Pandey (2008), Indian Government and Politics, Sage Publication: New Delhi, p.269.
3. Norman D. Plamer (1978), The Indian Political System, Houghton Mifflin: Boston, p.104.
4. Sandhu G.S, Kumar, Manoj, Local Government: Rural and Urban (Anmol Publications, New Delhi 2004), p. 65
5. B.L.Fadia (2009), Indian Government and Politics, Sahitya Bhawan Publication: Agra, p.506
6. Iqbal Narayan (1989), "Revival of Panchayati Raj", in B.C. Shah and J.N. Pandya (ed.) Revival of Panchayati Raj, Vallabh Vidyanagar: Bombay, pp-3-4
7. K.K.Ghai (2004), Indian Polity, Kalyani Publishers: Ludhiana, p.226
8. Ministry of Rural Development 2005, p. 1
9. Ministry of Rural Development 2012, p. ix
10. The Times of India 2013
11. Ibid, p.227
12. Ministry of Housing and Urban Poverty Alleviation, Government of India.
13. A. P. J. Abdul Kalam, Developing India Conference: Providing Urban Amenities in Rural Areas (PURA) - Conceptualisation, Impact, Assessment and Implementation Issues, Volume I, Issue 4 January-March 2010.
14. SRS Bulletin, Sample Registration System, Registar General, India; Volume 45 No.1; January 2011.
15. K. C. Sivaramakrishnan; Biplab Dasgupta; Mahesh N. Buch, *Urbanisation in India: Basic Services and People's Participation.* Concept Publishing Company, New Delhi, 2012, p. 2.
16. "AUICK Newsletter No. 27". Auick.org. 2012 .
17. Niu, Tong, "Problems of Urbanisation in India", 2011
18. Javir, "Problems of Urbanisation in India", Preserve Articles, 2012.

REFERENCES

C. Chakrapani and Arup Mitra(1995),"Rural to Urban Migration: Access to Employment

Incidence of Poverty and Determinants of Mobility", *Indian Journal of Social Work*, Vol.54, No.3, July, pp.377-86

M.Lingaraju and Johnson Samuel (2005), "Rural - Urban Linkages: Does Impermanent Migration to Cities help the Rural Poor? *Nagarlok*, Vol.37, No.1, Jan-March, pp.9-20

Mathur Om Prakash, "Alleviating Urban Poverty: Income Growth, Income Distribution, or Decentralisation?" in *India Urban Poverty Report: 2009,* New Delhi, Oxford University Press, 2009.

Hashim, S.R. "Economic Development & Urban Poverty", in *India Urban Poverty*

Report: 2009: New Delhi: Oxford University Press, 2009.

Meera Mehta and Dinesh Mehta, "Glass Half Full? Urban Development (1990-2010)", *Economic and Political Weekly*, XLV, No.28, July, 10, 2010, pp. 20-23.

5

INSTITUTIONAL INITIATIVES TOWARDS GOOD GOVERNANCE

DR. SUNITA MANGLA

RIGHT TO INFORMATION: (RTI)

The Right to Information Act (RTI) is an Act of Indian Parliament "to provide for setting out the practical regime of right to information for citizens" and to replace the erstwhile Freedom of Information Act, 2002. The Act applies to all States and Union Territories of India except Jammu & Kashmir. Under the provisions of the Act, any citizen may request information from a "public authority" (a body of Government or "instrumentality of State") which is required to reply expeditiously or within thirty days. The Act also requires every public authority to computerize their records for wide dissemination and to proactively certain categories of information so that the citizens need minimum recourse to request for information formally. This law was passed by Parliament on 15 June 2005 and came fully into force on 13 October 2005. Information disclosure in India was restricted by the Official Secrets Act 1923 and various other special laws, which the new RTI Act relaxes. RTI is an Act to provide for setting out the practical regime of right to information for citizens to secure access to information under the control of public authorities, in order to promote transparency and accountability in the working of every public authority, the constitution of a Central Information Commission and State

* Assistant Professor, Deptt. of Political Science, Kalindi College, Univ. of Delhi

Information Commissions and for matters connected therewith or incidental thereto.

The right to information is implicitly guaranteed by the Constitution. However, with a view to set out a practical regime for securing information, the Indian Parliament enacted the Right to Information Act, 2005 and thus gave a powerful tool to the citizens to get information from the Government as a matter of right. This law is very comprehensive and covers almost all matters of governance and has the widest possible reach, being applicable to Government at all levels- Union, State and Local as well as recipients of government grants. The Act requires the Government to compile a guide in easily comprehensible form and to update it from time to time. The Government has already published four guides in the past, one each for the information seekers, the public authorities, the Central Public Information Officers and the Appellate Authorities. Here is an updated consolidated guide for the use of all stake-holders. This guide contains five parts. Part I of the guide discusses some aspects of the Act which all the stake-holder are required to know. Rest of the four parts are specifically relevant to the public authorities, the information seekers, the public information officers and the first appellate authorities respectively. Contents of this guide are specifically relevant in relation to the Central Government but are equally applicable to the State Governments except in relation to rules about payment of fee or deciding of appeals by the Information Commissions. It may be noted that this guide uses the term Public Information Officer in place of Central Public Information Officer/State Public Information Officer. Likewise Assistant Public Information Officer has been used for Central Assistant Public Information Officer/State Assistant Public Information Officer.

Areas Not Covered Under RTI

The Act covers the whole of India except Jammu and Kashmir, where J&K Right to Information Act is in force. It is no to all constitutional authorities, including the executive, legislature and judiciary; any institution or body established or constituted by an act of Parliament or a state legislature. It is also defined in the Act that bodies or authorities established or constituted by order or notification of appropriate government including bodies "owned, controlled or substantially financed" by government, or non-Government organizations "substantially financed, directly or indirectly by funds" provided by the government are also covered in the Act. Private bodies are not within the Act's ambit directly. In a landmark decision of Sarbajit Roy versus Delhi Electricity Regulatory Commission, the Central Information Commission also reaffirmed that privatized public utility companies continue to be within the RTI Act- their privatization notwithstanding.

Central Intelligence and Security agencies specified in the Second Schedule like IB, Directorate General of Income tax(Investigation), RAW, Central Bureau of Investigation (CBI), Directorate of Revenue Intelligence, Central Economic Intelligence Bureau, Directorate of Enforcement, Narcotics Control Bureau, Aviation Research Centre, Special Frontier Force, BSF, CRPF, ITBP, CISF, NSG, Assam Rifles, Special Service Bureau, Special Branch (CID), Andaman and Nicobar, The Crime Branch-CID-CB, Dadra and Nagar Haveli and Special Branch, Lakshadweep Police. Agencies specified by the State Governments through a Notification will also be excluded. The exclusion, however, is not absolute and these organizations have an obligation to provide information pertaining to allegations of corruption and human rights violations. Further, information relating to allegations of human rights violation could be given but only with the approval of the Central or State Information Commission

The Central Information Commission (CIC) has held that the political parties are public authorities and answerable to citizens under RTI Act. The CIC, a quasi-judicial body, has said that six national parties:- Congress, BJP, NCP, CPI(M), CPI and BSP and BJD have been substantially funded indirectly by the Central Government and they have the character of public authority under the RTI Act as they perform public functions. On 12 August 2013, the Congress Party tabled RTI Amendment Bill 2013 in Lok Sabha to keep political parties out of RTI ambit.

The Bill to amend the Act so as to keep political parties out of its ambit, was on September 3, 2013 deferred to the Winter Session of Parliament. On December 17, 2013 the Standing Committee on Law and Personnel said in its report tabled in Parliament-*"The committee considers the proposed amendment is a right step to address the issue once and for all. The committee, therefore, recommends for passing of the Bill,"*.

Information Exclusions

The following is exempt from disclosure under section 8 of the Act:

- Information, disclosure of which would prejudicially affect the sovereignty and integrity of India, the security, "strategic, scientific or economic" interests of the State, relation with foreign State or lead to incitement of an offense;
- Information which has been expressly forbidden to be published by any court of law or tribunal or the disclosure of which may constitute contempt of court;
- Information, the disclosure of which would cause a breach of privilege of Parliament or the State Legislature;
- Information including commercial confidence, trade secrets or intellectual property, the disclosure of which would harm the competitive position of a third party, unless the competent authority is satisfied that larger public interest warrants the disclosure of such information;
- Information available to a person in his fiduciary relationship, unless the competent authority is satisfied that the larger public interest warrants the disclosure of such information;
- Information received in confidence from foreign Government;
- Information, the disclosure of which would endanger the life or physical safety of any person or identify the source of information

or assistance given in confidence for law enforcement or security purposes;

- Information which would impede the process of investigation or apprehension or prosecution of offenders;
- Cabinet papers including records of deliberations of the Council of Ministers, Secretaries and other officers;
- Information which relates to personal information the disclosure of which has no relationship to any public activity or interest, or which would cause unwarranted invasion of the privacy of the individual (but it is also provided that the information which cannot be denied to the Parliament or a State Legislature shall not be denied by this exemption);
- Notwithstanding any of the exemptions listed above, a public authority may allow access to information, if public interest in disclosure outweighs the harm to the protected interests. However, this does not apply to disclosure of "trade or commercial secrets protected by law ".

Central Information Commission: The Central Information Commission was established by the Central Government in 2005. It was constituted through an official Gazette Notification under the provisions of the Right to Information Act (2005). Therefore, it is not a constitutional body.

Composition: The Commission consists of a Chief Information Commissioner and not more than ten Information Commissioners. They appointed by the president on the recommendation of a committee consisting of the Prime Minister as Chairperson, the leader of Opposition in the Lok Sabha and a Union Cabinet Minister nominated by the Prime Minister. They should be persons of eminence in public life with wide knowledge and experience in law, science and technology, social service, management, journalism, mass media or administration and governance. They should not be a member of Parliament or Member of the Legislature of any state or Union Territory. They should not hold any other office of profit or connected with any political party or carrying on any business or pursuing any profession.

Tenure: The Chief Information Commissioner and an Information Commissioner hold office for a term of 5 years or until they attain the age of 65 years, whichever is earlier. They are not eligible for reappointment. But the Information Commissioner is eligible for appointment as chief Information Commissioner but cannot hold office for more than a total of five years including his term as Information Commissioner.

Powers and Functions: The powers and functions of Central Information Commission are-

1. It is duty of the Commission to receive and inquire into a complaint from any person.
2. The Commission can order inquiry into any matter if there are reasonable grounds (suo-moto-power).
3. While inquiring , the Commission has the power of a civil court.
4. All public records must be given to the commission during inquiry for examination.
5. The Commission has the power to secure compliance of its decisions from the public authority.
6. The Commission submits an annual report to the Central Government on the implementation of the provisions of this Act. The Central Government places this report before each House of Parliament.
7. When a public authority does not conform to the provisions of this Act, the Commission may recommend steps which ought to be taken for promoting such conformity.

HOW TO FILE RTI

The RTI process involves reactive (as opposed to proactive) disclosure of information by the authorities. An RTI request initiates the process.

Each authority covered by the RTI Act must appoint their **Public Information Officer** (PIO). Any person may submit a written request to the PIO for information. It is the PIO's obligation to provide information to citizens of India who request information under the Act. If the request pertains to another public authority (in whole or part), it is the PIO's responsibility to transfer/forward the concerned portions of the request to a PIO of the other authority within 5 working days. In addition, every public authority is required to designate **Assistant Public Information Officers** (APIOs) to receive RTI requests and appeals for forwarding to the PIOs of their public authority. The applicant is required to disclose his name and contact particulars but not any other reasons or justification for seeking information.

The Central Information Commission (CIC) acts upon complaints from those individuals who have not been able to submit information requests to a Central Public Information Officer or State Public Information Officer due to either the officer not having been appointed, or because the respective Central Assistant Public Information Officer or State Assistant Public Information Officer refused to receive the application for information.

The Act specifies time limits for replying to the request.

- If the request has been made to the PIO, the reply is to be given within **30 days** of receipt.
- If the request has been made to an APIO, the reply is to be given within **35 days** of receipt.
- If the PIO transfers the request to another public authority (better concerned with the information requested), the time allowed to reply is **30 days** but computed from the day after it is received by the PIO of the transferee authority.
- Information concerning corruption and Human Rights violations by scheduled Security agencies (those listed in the Second Schedule to the Act) is to be provided within **45 days** but with the prior approval of the Central Information Commission.
- However, if life or liberty of any person is involved, the PIO is expected to reply within **48 hours**.

Since the information is to be paid for, the reply of the PIO is necessarily limited to either denying the request (in whole or part) and/or providing a computation of "further fees". The time between the reply of the PIO and the time taken to deposit the further fees for information is excluded from the time allowed. If information is not provided within this period, it is treated as deemed refusal. Refusal with or without reasons may be ground for appeal or complaint. Further, information not provided in the times prescribed is to be provided free of charge. Appeal processes are also defined.

Figure:1 Time Limits for Replying to the Request (according to the conditions involved)

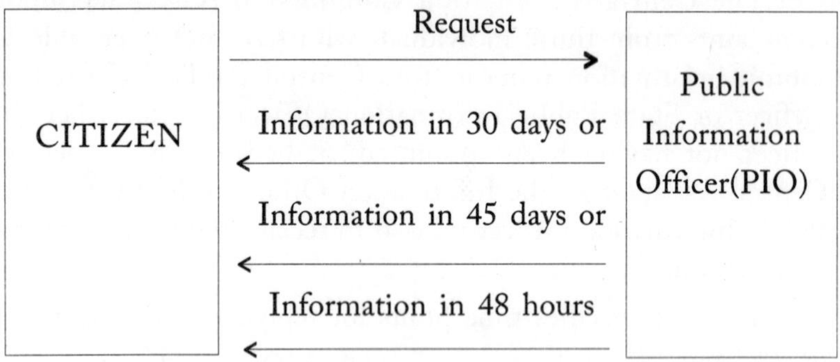

Source: RTI ACT

Fee for Seeking Information

A person who desires to seek some information from a public authority is required to send, along with the application, a demand draft or a banker's cheque or an Indian Postal Order of Rs. 10/- (Rupees ten), payable to the Accounts Officer of the public authority as fee prescribed for seeking information. The payment of fee can also be made by way of cash to the Accounts Officer of the public authority or to the Assistant Public Information Officer against proper receipt. The applicant may also be required to pay further fee towards the cost of providing the information, details of which shall be intimated to the applicant by the PIO as prescribed by the Right to Information (Regulation of Fee and Cost) Rules, 2005. Rates of fee as prescribed in the Rules are given below:

(a) Rupees two (Rs. 2/-) for each page (in A-4 or A-3 size paper) created or copied;

(b) Actual charge or cost price of a copy in larger size paper;

(c) Actual cost or price for samples or models;

(d) For information provided in diskette or floppy, rupees fifty (Rs. 50/-) per diskette or floppy; and

(e) For information provided in printed form, at the price fixed for such Publication or rupees two per page of photocopy for extracts from the Publication.

As already pointed out, a citizen has a right to inspect the records of a public authority. For inspection of records, the public authority shall charge no fee for the first hour. But a fee of rupees five (Rs. 5/-) for each subsequent hour (or fraction thereof) shall be charged.

If the applicant belongs to below poverty line (BPL) category, he is not required to pay any fee. However, he should submit a proof in support of his claim to belong to the below poverty line. The application not accompanied by the prescribed fee of Rs. 10/- or proof of the applicant's belonging to below poverty line, as the case may be, shall not be a valid application under the Act. It may be pointed out that there is no bar on the public authority to supply information in response to such applications. However, provisions of Act would not apply to such cases.There is no prescribed format of application for seeking information. The application can be made on plain paper. The application should, however, have the name and complete postal address of the applicant. Even in cases where the information is sought electronically, the application should contain name and postal address of the applicant.

Filing of Appeal

An applicant can file an appeal to the first appellate authority if information is not supplied to him within the prescribed time of thirty days or 48 hours, as the case may be, or is not satisfied with the information furnished to him. Such an appeal, should be filed within a period of thirty days from the date on which the limit of 30 days of supply of information is expired or from the date on which the information or decision of the Public Information Officer is received. The appellate authority of the public authority shall dispose of the appeal within a period of thirty days or in exceptional cases within 45 days of the receipt of the appeal.

If the appellate authority fails to pass an order on the appeal within the prescribed period or if the appellant is not satisfied with the order of the first appellate authority, he may prefer a second appeal with the Information Commission within ninety days from the date on which the decision should have been made by the first appellate authority or was actually received by the appellant.

The appeal made to the Central Information Commission should contain the following information:

(i) Name and address of the appellant;

(ii) Name and address of the Public Information Officer against the decision of whom the appeal is preferred;

(iii) Particulars of the order including number, if any, against which the appeal is preferred;

(iv) Brief facts leading to the appeal;

(v) If the appeal is preferred against deemed refusal, particulars of the application, including number and date and name and address of the Public Information Officer to whom the application was made;

(vi) Prayer or relief sought;

(v) Grounds for prayer or relief;

(vi) Verification by the appellant; and

(vii) Any other information, which the Commission may deem necessary for deciding the appeal.

The appeal made to the Central Information Commission should be accompanied by the following documents:

(i) Self-attested copies of the orders or documents against which appeal is made;

(ii) Copies of the documents relied upon by the appellant and referred to in the appeal; and

(iii) An index of the documents referred to in the appeal.

CITIZEN'S CHARTER

Citizen's Charter is a document which represents a systematic effort to focus on the commitment of the Organization towards its Citizens in respects of Standard of Services, Information, Choice and Consultation, Non-discrimination and Accessibility, Grievance Redress, Courtesy and Value for Money. This also includes expectations of the Organization from the Citizen for fulfilling the commitment of the Organization.

A Citizens' Charter represents the commitment of an organization towards standard, quality and time frame of service delivery, grievance redressal mechanism, transparency and accountability. Based on the anticipated expectations and aspirations of public, Citizens' Charters are to be drawn-up with care and concern for the concerned service users. They enable the service seekers to avail the services of the government departments with minimum inconvenience and maximum speed. For this, the Citizens' Charters are expected to indicate 'WHERE TO GO' and 'HOW TO PROCEED'. On the other hand, it makes the service providers aware of their duties to attend to the problems of the concerned citizens within a reasonable time-frame. Thus, the dissemination of information about the Charter's contents for the awareness and sense of responsibility & accountability among all are the keys to practical application of Citizens' Charter in any area.

The term 'Citizen' in the Citizen's Charter implies the clients or customers whose interests and values are addressed by the Citizen's Charter and, therefore, includes not only the citizens but also all the stakeholders, i.e., citizens, customers, clients, users, beneficiaries, other Ministries/ Departments/ Organizations, State Governments, UT Administrations etc.

Basic Concept, Origin and Principles

It has been recognised world over that good governance is essential for sustainable development, both economic and social. The three essential aspects emphasised in good governance are transparency, accountability and responsiveness of the administration. "Citizen's Charters" initiative is a response to the quest for solving the problems which a citizen encounters, day in and day out, while dealing with the organizations providing public services. The concept of Citizen's Charter enshrines the trust between the service provider and its users. The concept was first articulated and implemented in the United Kingdom by the Conservative Government of John Major in 1991 as a National Programme with a simple aim: to continuously improve the quality of public services for the people of the country so that these services respond to the needs and wishes of the users. The programme was re-launched in 1998 by the Labour Government of Tony Blair which rechristened it "**Service First**". The basic objective of the Citizen's Charter

is to empower the citizen in relation to public service delivery.

The six principles of the Citizen's Charter movement as originally framed were:

(i) **Quality**: Improving the quality of services;

(ii) **Choice:** Providing choice wherever possible;

(iii) **Standards**: Specify what to expect and how to act if standards are not met;

(iv) **Value**: Add value for the taxpayers' money;

(v) **Accountability**: Be accountable to individuals and organizations;

(vi) **Transparency**: Ensure transparency in Rules/Procedures/Schemes/Grievances.

These were later elaborated by the Labour Government as following nine principles of Service Delivery (1998):

- Set standards of service
- Be open and provide full information
- Consult and involve
- Encourage access and the promotion of choice
- Treat all fairly
- Put things right when they go wrong
- Use resources effectively
- Innovate and improve
- Work with other providers.

International Movement for Citizen's Charter

The UK's Citizen's Charter initiative aroused considerable interest around the world and several countries implemented similar programmes e.g., Australia (Service Charter, 1997),Belgium(Public Service Users' Charter 1992), Canada (Service Standards Initiative, 1995), France (Service Charter, 1992), India (Citizen's Charter, 1997), Jamaica (Citizen's Charter 1994), Malaysia (Client Charter, 1993), Portugal (The Quality Charter in Public Services, 1993), and Spain (The Quality Observatory, 1992) (OECD, 1996). Some of these initiatives are very similar to the UK model, while others chart new ground by leaning on the service quality paradigm of the Total Quality Management (TQM) movement.

Other initiatives are pitched somewhere in between. Even in the UK, in the context of the Next Steps/Modernising Government Initiatives, Citizen's Charters have acquired a service quality face for delivery of public services. The quality tools adopted for improving public services include the Business Excellence Model, Investors in People, Charter Mark, ISO 9000 and Best Value (Government of UK, 1999). The Government of Malaysia issued Guidelines on the Client's Charter in 1993 to assist government agencies to prepare and implement Client's Charter, which is "a written commitment by an agency to deliver outputs or services according to specified standards of quality"

(Government of Malaysia, 1998). A Best Client's Charter Award was instituted in 1993.

The Malaysian system of Client's Charter closely follows the UK Model. A distinction is made between agency-wide and unit charters. The concept of 'service recovery' enjoins taking steps to restore the trust and confidence of the client in a proactive manner when things go wrong.

The Commonwealth Government of Australia launched its Service Charter initiative in 1997 as part of its on-going commitment to improve the quality of service provided by agencies to the Australian community by moving the government organisation away from bureaucratic processes to customer-focused outcomes. Service Charters are considered a powerful tool for fostering change and require the organisation to focus on services delivered, to measure and assess performance, and to initiate performance improvement. By providing goals for agencies to strive towards, a Charter acts as a surrogate for competition where none exists (Department of Finance and Administration, 1999). Centre link is a one-stop shop that provides access to Australian government services for over six million customers. Centre link has adopted one-to-one service as an innovative and personalized approach to service delivery. One-to-one service treats customers with respect and consistency and takes the complexity out of dealing with government.

The Treasury Board of Canada Secretariat started a Service Standard Initiative in 1995 which took its cue from the Citizen's Charters of the United Kingdom, but enlarged the scope considerably. This Service Standard Initiative in Canada was started against the backdrop of citizen expectations relating to friendly, respectful and courteous service; faster response times; extended hours at government offices; and "one-stop-shopping". At the same time there was a need to reduce the deficit and provide value for money through more efficient use of resources (Treasury Board of Canada, 1995). A comparison of these four major Citizen's Charter initiatives shows that the service quality approach is embedded in them in different degrees. Once adecision is taken to make public services citizen-centric, the customer focus of the Total Quality Management (TQM) variety cannot be far behind. In fact, the Citizen's Charter approach has several things in common with TQM. Both begin by focusing on meeting customer/citizen requirements. Other key common elements are conformance to standards, stakeholder involvement and continuous improvement.

The Indian Experience of Citizen's Charter

Over the years, in India, significant progress has been made in the field of economic development. This, along with a substantial increase in the literacy rate, (from 51.63% to 65.38% in the last decade) has made Indian citizens increasingly aware of their rights. Citizens have become more articulate and expect the administration not merely to respond to their demands but also to anticipate them. It was in this climate that since 1996 a consensus had evolved in the Government on effective and responsive administration. In a Conference of Chief Ministers of various States and Union Territories held on 24 May, 1997 in New Delhi, presided over by the Prime Minister of India, an "Action Plan for Effective and Responsive Government" at the Centre and State levels was adopted. One of the major decisions at that Conference was that the Central and State Governments would formulate Citizens' Charters, starting with those sectors that have a large public interface (e.g. Railways, Telecom, Posts, Public Distribution Systems). These Charters were required to include standards of service and time limits that the public can reasonably expect, avenues of grievance redress and a provision for independent scrutiny with the involvement of citizen and consumer groups.

Department of Administrative Reforms and Public Grievances in Government of India (DARPG) initiated the task of coordinating, formulating and operationalising Citizens' Charters. Guidelines for formulating the Charters as well as a list of do's and don'ts were communicated to various government departments/organisations to enable them to bring out focused and effective charters. For the formulation of the Charters, the government agencies at the Centre and State levels were advised to constitute a task force with representation from users, senior management and the cutting edge staff. A Handbook on Citizen's Charter has been developed by the Department and sent to all the State Governments/UT Administrations.

The Charters are expected to incorporate the following elements:

(i) Vision and Mission Statement;

(ii) Details of business transacted by the organisation;

(iii) Details of clients;

(iv) Details of services provided to each client group;

(v) Details of grievance redress mechanism and how to access it; and

(vi) Expectations from the clients.

Primarily an adaptation of the UK model, the Indian Citizens' Charter has an additional component of 'expectations from the clients' or in other words 'obligations of the users'. Involvement of consumer organisations, citizen groups, and other stakeholders in the formulation of the Citizens' Charter is emphasised to ensure that the Citizens' Charter meets the needs of the users. Regular monitoring, review and evaluation of the Charters, both internally and through external agencies, are enjoined. Till April, 2006, 111 Citizens' Charters had been formulated by the Central Government Ministries/ Departments/ Organisations and 668 Charters by various agencies of State Governments & Administrations of Union Territories. Most of the national Charters are posted on the government's websites and are open to public scrutiny. The organisations with Citizens' Charters are advised to give publicity to their Charters through such means as print/ electronic media and awareness campaigns.

Implementation of Citizen's Charter in India

While the overall efforts and initiatives of the government on Citizens' Charter were continuing, it was realised that exemplary implementation of the Charter in a major public interface area of government would not only establish the new concept in the inertia-prone bureaucracy but also act as a role model for replication in other sectors/areas. The banking sector was identified for this purpose keeping in view the second phase of economic reforms and the fact that this sector was fairly advanced in terms of customer service and was also taking advantage of information technology to speed up various processes. The primary objective of this exercise was to build the Banking Sector as a model of excellence in the implementation of the Citizens' Charter.

To begin with, three major National level Banks, namely, Punjab National Bank, Punjab and Sind Bank and Oriental Bank of Commerce, were selected for a Hand-Holding exercise by the DARPG in the year 2000. The following key issues were highlighted for exemplary implementation of the Citizens' Charter :-

(i) stakeholder involvement in the formulation of Citizens' Charters;

(ii) deployment of the Citizens' Charters in the Banks by full involvement of the staff, specially the employees at the cutting-edge level;

(iii) creation of awareness about the Charter amongst the customers of the Banks; and

(iv) special training for employees at all levels about the concept and implementation of Citizens' Charter.

After an evaluation of the current status of the Charters by the identified banks through independent agencies, Action Plans were chalked out to rectify shortcomings. The Charters were, accordingly, revised and standardised on the basis of the model/mother Charter developed by the Indian Banks Association (IBA). Training for employees of selected branches through master trainers, trained by the National Institute of Bank Management using a module developed in consultation with Department of ARPG were organised. Several measures to give wide publicity to Citizens' Charter were also undertaken.

An external agency was engaged to once again assess and evaluate the implementation of Citizens' Charter of these banks at the end of this exercise and also to document the Hand-Holding Exercise. National Institute of Bank Management was assigned this task which had since been executed and a documentation was brought out in the Year 2003.

Evaluation of Citizens' Charters

An evaluation of the Citizens' Charters of various government agencies was carried out by DARPG and Consumer Coordination Council, New Delhi, an NGO, in October 1998. The results were quite encouraging given the nascent stage of this initiative in India. A brief questionnaire has been circulated to all Ministries/Departments and State Governments/Union Territories to enable them to undertake an in-house evaluation of their Citizens' Charters. Organisations have also been advised to undertake external evaluations, preferably through NGOs.

During the Year 2002-03, DARPG engaged a professional agency to develop a standardised model for internal and external evaluation of Citizens' Charters in a more effective, quantifiable and objective manner. This agency also carried out evaluation of implementation of Charters in 5 Central Government Organisations and 15 Departments/ Organisations of States of Andhra Pradesh, Maharashtra and Uttar Pradesh. This Agency was also required to suggest methods for increasing awareness, both within the organisation and among the users, and to suggest possible methods for orientation of management and the staff in the task of formulating and deploying Charters.

As per the report of evaluation carried out by the Agency, major findings were:

(i) In majority of cases Charters were not formulated through a consultative process;

(ii) By and large service providers are not familiar with the philosophy, goals and main features of the Charter;

(iii) Adequate publicity to the Charters had not been given in any of the Departments evaluated. In most Departments, the Charters are only in the initial or middle stage of implementation;

(iv) No funds have been specifically earmarked for awareness generation of Citizens' Charter or for orientation of staff on various components of the Charter;

Key recommendations, inter alia, include:

(i) need for citizens and staff to be consulted at every stage of formulation of the Charter,

(ii) Orientation of staff about the salient features and goals/ objectives of the Charter; vision and mission statement of the department; ¬d skills such as team building, problem solving, handling of grievances and communication skills,

(iii) Need for creation of database on consumer grievances and redress,

(iv) Need for wider publicity of the Charter through print media, posters, banners, leaflets, handbills, brochures, local newspapers etc. and also through electronic media,

(v) Earmarking of specific budgets for awareness generation and orientation of staff, and

(vi) Replication of best practices in this field.

Problems faced in Implementing the Charters

As pointed out, the Citizens' Charters initiative in India had started in 1997 and the Charters formulated are in a nascent stage of implementation. Introduction of a new concept is always difficult in any organisation. Introduction and implementation of the concept of Citizens' Charter in the Government of India was much more difficult due to the old bureaucratic set up/ procedures and the rigid attitudes of the work force. The major obstacles encountered in this initiative were:

1. The general perception of organisations which formulated Citizens' Charters was that the exercise was to be carried out because there was a direction from the top. The consultation process was minimal or largely absent. It thus became one of the routine activities of the organisation and had no focus.

2. For any Charter to succeed, the employees responsible for its implementation should have proper training and orientation, as commitments of the Charter cannot be expected to be delivered by a workforce that is unaware of the spirit and content of the Charter. However, in many cases, the concerned staff were not adequately trained and sensitised.
3. Sometimes, transfers and reshuffles of concerned officers at the crucial stages of formulation/implementation of a Citizens' Charter in an organisation severely undermined the strategic processes which were put in place and hampered the progress of the initiative.
4. Awareness campaigns to educate clients about the Charter were not conducted systematically.
5. In some cases, the standards/time norms of services mentioned in Citizens' Charter were either too lax or too tight and were, therefore, unrealistic and created an unfavourable impression on the clients of the Charter.
6. The concept behind the Citizens' Charter was not properly understood. Information brochures, publicity materials, pamphlets produced earlier by the organisations were mistaken for Citizens' Charters.

According to a study undertaken by Transparency International India, in May 2002 about the degree of application of the Citizens' Charters in respect of eleven Departments of Delhi Govt. and two Central Government Departments, namely, DDA and Income Tax the following problem areas were identified :

1. Lack of awareness and knowledge and adequate publicity, hence loss of trust among service seekers.
2. No training to the operative and supervisory staff.
3. Lack of infrastructure and initiative.
4. Hierarchy gap between the Officers and the Operative Staff- Need of team effort.

5. Different mind-sets of officers and the Staff- Insensitiveness on the part of the Supervisors and the Staff because they are yet to be sensitized.
6. Staff is not prepared to shoulder the responsibility due to lack of motivation and accountability.
7. Non-revision, complicated and restrictive rules & procedures.

Lessons Learnt

The following lessons have been learnt from the experience to date of implementing Citizens' Charter initiative:

1. As with any new effort, the Citizens' Charter initiative is bound to be looked at initially with skepticism by bureaucrats as well as citizens. An effective awareness campaign amongst all the stakeholders at the initial stage is essential to overcome this skepticism. These awareness campaigns should be designed and delivered innovatively and effectively.
2. The issuance of Citizens' Charter will not change overnight the mindset of the staff and the clients, developed over a period of time. Therefore, regular, untiring and persistent efforts are required to bring about the attitudinal changes.
3. A new initiative always encounters barriers and misgivings from the staff. There is a natural resistance to change, particularly among the cutting-edge staff. Involving and consulting them at all the levels of formulation and implementation of Citizens' Charter will go a long way in overcoming this resistance and will make them an equal partner in this exercise.
4. Instead of trying to reform all the processes at once and encounter massive resistance, it is advisable to break it into small components and tackle them one at a time.
5. The charter initiative should have an built-in mechanism for monitoring, evaluating and reviewing the working of the Charters, preferably through an outside agency.

Future Vision: Development of Charter Mark

In 1992, the UK Government introduced Charter Mark, a scheme for recognising and encouraging excellence in public service. To win a Charter Mark the organisation has to demonstrate excellence against the following nine Charter Mark criteria which correspond to the principles of public service delivery, namely,

(1) Performance Standards;

(2) Information and openness;

(3) Choice and Consultation;

(4) Courtesy and helpfulness;

(5) Putting things right;

(6) Value for money;

(7) Use satisfaction;

(8) Improvements in service quality; and

(9) Planned improvements and innovations. The Government of Malaysia also instituted a "Best Client's Charter Award" in 1993 based on the UK model.

In India, the DARPG has identified a professional agency to develop an appropriate Charter Mark scheme. This scheme will encourage and reward improvement in public service delivery with reference to the commitments and standards notified in the Charter. The 'Charter Mark' is proposed to be awarded after assessment by an independent panel of judges. This would not only give a sense of achievement to the organisation awarded the Charter Mark but also promote a spirit of competitiveness amongst various organisations that have issued Citizens' Charter and generating awareness among citizens. A prototype has been developed by the professional agency and is in the process of validation in identified Departments/ Organisations.

The implementation of Citizens' Charter is an on-going exercise because it has to reflect the extensive and continual changes taking place in the domain of public services. Indian

Government continuously strives to serve the citizens in an effective and efficient way so as not only to meet but to exceed their expectations. The Citizens' Charter initiative is a major step in this direction.

CONSUMER RIGHTS

Meaning

The definition of Consumer right is 'the right to have information about the quality, potency, quantity, purity, price and standard of goods or services', as it may be the case, but the consumer is to be protected against any unfair practices of trade. It is very essential for the consumers to know these rights. Consumer protection is a group of laws and organizations designed to ensure the rights of consumers as well as fair trade competition and the free flow of truthful information in the marketplace. The laws are designed to prevent businesses that engage in fraud or specified unfair practices from gaining an advantage over competitors; they may also provide additional protection for the weak and those unable to take care of themselves. Consumer protection laws are a form of government regulation, which aim to protect the rights of consumers. For example, a government may require businesses to disclose detailed information about products- particularly in areas where safety or public health is an issue, such as food. Consumer protection is linked to the idea of consumer rights, and to the formation of consumer organizations, which help consumers make better choices in the marketplace and get help with consumer complaints.

Other organizations that promote consumer protection include government organizations and self-regulating business organizations such as consumer protection agencies and organizations, the Federal Trade Commission, ombudsmen, Better Business Bureaus, etc. A consumer is defined as someone who acquires goods or services for direct use or ownership rather than for resale or use in production and manufacturing. Consumer interests can also be protected by promoting competition in the markets which directly and indirectly serve consumers, consistent with economic efficiency, but this topic is treated in competition law. Consumer protection can also be asserted via non-government organizations and individuals as consumer activism.

However there are strong and clear laws in India to defend consumer rights, the actual plight of consumers of India can be declared as completely dismal. Out of the various laws that have been enforced to protect the consumer rights in India, the most important is the Consumer Protection Act, 1986. According to this law, everybody, including individuals, a firm, a Hindu undivided family and a company, have the right to exercise their consumer rights for the purchase of goods and services made by them. It is significant that, as consumer, one knows the basic rights as well as about the courts and procedures that follow with the infringement of one's rights.

THE MAJOR RIGHTS FOR CONSUMERS

The main rights of consumers are as follows:

1. Right to safety:

Consumers have the right to be protected against the marketing of goods which are hazardous to life and health. Food additives and colours, dangerous toys, flammable fabrics, unsafe appliances are examples of such goods. Consumers are entitled to healthy and safe products.

2. Right to information:

It means the right to be informed about the quality, quantity, potency, purity, standard and the price of goods so as to protect the consumers against unfair trade practices.

3. Right to choose:

Consumers must have access to a variety of goods at competitive prices. Free competition and wide variety enable consumers to choose the best goods.

4. Right to be heard:

Consumers need to be assured that their interests will receive due consideration at appropriate forums.

5. Right to education:

Consumers have the right to be made aware of their rights and remedies available to them for redressal of their grievances.

6. Right to redressal:

Standing machinery must be provided for quick and satisfactory redressal of consumer grievances against unfair trade practices and exploitation by unscrupulous elements.

7. Right to healthy environment:

Consumers have the right to live in a pollution free environment. This is necessary to enhance the quality of human life.

METHODS OF CONSUMER PROTECTION

The following methods can be adopted for protection of consumers.

1. Self-regulation by business:

Business exists to serve consumers. There is a growing realisation that business should provide good quality products at reasonable prices. Businessmen should regulate their behaviour by adopting just and fair trade practices.

They should avoid the temptation to make money by cheating customers. Trade associations and chambers of commerce should enforce discipline among businessmen through codes of conduct and regulations.

2. Consumer Association:

Consumers themselves should insist on value for money spent and ensure their rights. They should organise and unite by forming consumer associations.

Common cause, VOICE, Grahak Panchayat are examples of such associations in India. They are edu-cating consumers and protecting their rights. "Self help is the best help".

3. Consumerism:

According to Philip Kotler, "consumerism is an organised movement of citizens and Government to strengthen the rights and powers of buyers in relation to seller".

Consumerism is a social force aimed at protecting the consumers by exerting moral and economic pressure on business community. It is an organised movement of consumers.

The Government of India has taken several measures to promote a strong and broad-based consumer movement in the country. It has instituted National Awards for consumer protection and provides financial assistance to consumers' organisations.

The Consumers' Welfare Funds Scheme 1992 is meant to provide financial assistance to protect and promote the welfare of the consumers. It prepares and distributes audiovisual materials on consumer affairs.

March 15 every year is celebrated as World Consumer Rights Day. Radio and Doordarshan carry programmes regularly on consumer protection.

A quarterly journal UPBHOKTA, JAGRAN and several book-lets are published to educate consumers. The Bureau of India Standards is preparing and imple-menting quality standards and certification schemes.

4. Legislative measures:

Government of India has taken several legislative measures for the protection of consumers. Some of the legislative measures are as under:

(a) The Sale of Goods Act, 1930

(b) The Agriculture Produce (Grading and Marketing) Act, 1937

(c) The Drugs and Cosmetics Act, 1948

(d) The Drugs Control Act, 1950

(e) The Drugs and Magic Remedies (Objectionable Advertisements) Act, 1953

(f) The Prevention of Food Adulteration Act, 1954

(g) The Essential Commodities Act, 1953

(h) The Standard of Weights and Measures Act, 1956

(i) The Trade and Merchandise Marks Act, 1958

(j) The Monopolies and Restrictive Trade Practices Act, 1969

(k) The Prevention of Black-marketing and Maintenance of Supplies of Essential Commodi-ties Act, 1980.

(l) The Consumer Protection Act, 1986

(m) The Indian Patents and Designs Act

(n) The Household Electrical Appliances (Quality control) Order, 1976.

THE CONSUMER PROTECTION ACT, 1986

The Consumer Protection Act came into force on July 1, 1987. It provides enormous powers to consumers and consumer organisations against unscrupulous businessmen.

Objects

The Consumer Protection Act seeks to provide speedy and inexpensive redressal to the grievances of consumers. It is designed to protect the rights and interests of consumers.

Consumer Rights

The Act recognizes the following rights of consumers:

i. The right to be protected against the marketing of goods which are hazardous to life and property.

ii. The right to be informed about the quality, quantity, potency, purity, standard and price of goods so as to protect the consumers against unfair trade practices.

iii. The right to have access to a variety of goods at competitive prices

iv. The right to be heard and to be assured that consumer interests will receive due consid-eration at appropriate forums.

v. The right to consumer education

vi. The right to seek redressal against unfair trade practices or unscrupulous exploitation of consumers.

JAGO GRAHAK JAGO AWARENESS

Consumer Protection Act, 1986 implied all those guidelines which United Nations has suggested for incorporation to ensure best Consumer Protection. It is undeniable fact that many such consumer movements are already working in the country with them spreading fast countrywide. The scenario has hardly changed today. It is indeed still in its primitive stage due to the consumer movements often failing to get success. They are usually confined to certain areas or relate to the consumer awareness levels. It is very much crucial to develop the awareness campaigns in whole country through giving proper education to consumers to understand their rights and the responsibilities as consumers. If taken into account the area-wise assessment of different localities in the country one finds too much gap in consumer awareness levels from one part of country to other. It all happened due to literacy and awareness levels of people in various states. It is a draconian task to educate more than 120 crore masses that too the representatives of several groups or categories. Difficulties are more in the rural regions because they are locations where consumers can be easily exploited on several stages in terms of consumer interests in departments or ministries concerned. Take for example allocation of Rs.409 crores to start effective multimedia campaigns for 11th plan scheme implementation. Unique brand name 'Jago Grahak Jago' is part of the scheme implemented today. Rs. 409.29 crores was allocated for the 12th plan scheme. **National Helpline: 1800 11 4000**

INDIAN OMBUDSMAN (LOKPAL AND LOKAYUKTAS)

WHAT IS AN OMBUDSMAN?

The institution of ombudsman was first conceived and put into operation in **Sweden**.

Swedish word meaning commissioner has proved to be very exportable after the Second World War. Ombudsman has become a reality in several countries and is an aspiration, a much talked about reform measure in others.The dictionary defines the ombudsman as "an official to investigate complaints by individual against maladministration by public authorities. Maladministration is a vague term but may broadly refer to the way in which something has been handled, for example unjustifiable delay incompetence, neglect or prejudice and not to the merits of the decision.

It may be taken to cover administrative action or inaction based on or influenced by improper considerations. Arbitrariness, malice or bias including unfair discrimination are examples of improper considerations. India is to reincarnate this functionary under the name of lokpal and is to use it as an anti-corruption institution.India has been talking about ombudsman more or less regularly since 1967. Given the name of **Lokpal**, the Administrative Reforms Commission (1966-70) under Morarji Desai, later K. Hanumanthaiya submitted its first report recommending the installation of this functionary.

The ARC recommended a two-tiered machinery comprising the Lokpal and the Lokagukta, the former to deal with complaints against Ministers and states. The Lokayukta, one for the centre and one for each state, should attend to complaints against the rest of the bureaucracy.

First, the Lokpal Bill mooted in 1968 in terms of the recommendations of the Administrative Reforms Commission, the Bill was revised in 1971, 1977, 1985, 1989, 1995 and 1996.

The Rajiv Gandhi Govt. brought forward the Lokpal Bill in 1985 only to drop it later. In July 1995 the Narsimha Rao

Govt. announced its intention to in act the Lokpal Bill. The Dove Gowda Govt. introduced the Lokpal Bill in the Loksabha in September 1996, which however lapsed with the dissolution of the Loksabha.

The Vajapayee Govt. has prepared its own Bill which one must add, marks an improvement on the earlier ones in many ways, It provides for a multi-member committee for the appointment of the Lokpal and the two members the Lokpal as proposed now is to be a three-member body.

The Congress was opposed to the idea of bringing the Chief executive within the purview of the Lokpal. The Narsimha Rao Govt. had shown its agreement not to exclude the chief Executive.

The Vajpayee Govt. enlarges the jurisdiction of the functionary. The proposed Bill envisages the setting up of the Lokpal to examine the charges of corruption leveled against the Prime Minister, the union council of ministers and members of parliament.

The Vajpayee Govt's Bill on Lokpal was first considered by the standing committee on Home Affairs. A broad-based body must recommend the name for the office. The time span for examination of charges by the Lokpal must not be unduly restricted.

The Lokpal should examine the charges covering up to a period of the previous ten years. The inquiry should not be conducted in camera but should be held on open. The elected members must declare to the Lokpal their assets within 90 days of the commencement of each financial year and annually thereafter within 90 days. Non-filing or delayed filing of returns or incomplete filing should be visited with deterrent punishment.

The Lokpal institution visualised in India is to be a three member body. These members must be absolutely independent and impartial as both the Prime Minister and the leader of opposition would be within its jurisdiction.It equally well known, that it is not easy in our courts to prove changes of corruption. The onus of proof must not rest with the accuser. Any such provision is surely to deter any one from invoking the Lokpal. Lastly, the Lokpal must be endowed with its independent investigative agency, the CBI being the hand maid of the ruling party.

In India, the Lokpal is visualised as the country's watch dog institution on ministerial probity but he can be effective only when Viewed as being part of the anti-corruption institutional frame work, its other parts being an autonomous central Bureau of Investigation, effective electoral and administrative reform, abrogation of section 1907 the prevention of corruption Act etc.

For the politician in India, no code of conduct has been formulated so far India does not yet have a regular machinery to book the corrupt politician one must, however, warn that the institution of Lokpal has a fruitful role to play in a system of government which habitually operates at a reasonably high level of integrity, efficiency and devotion.

The smaller the zone of administrative wrongs the Greater is the utility of Lokpal where corruptions is wide spread and efficiency low, the entire administration needs to be revamped, and this, institution is hardly a sufficient cure for such a state of affairs. The institution of Lokpal is not a substitute for administrative reform.

What powers do they have?

Ombudsmen have powers which help them in resolving client issues. These powers may vary from industry to industry. For example, an Insurance Ombudsman has two types of functions to perform — conciliation and award making. The Insurance Ombudsman is empowered to receive and consider complaints in respect of personal lines of insurance from any person who has any grievance against an insurer.

The complaint may relate to any grievance against the insurer i.e.

(a) any partial or total repudiation of claims by the insurance companies,

(b) dispute with regard to premium paid or payable in terms of the policy,

(c) dispute on the legal construction of the policy wordings in case such dispute relates to claims;

(d) delay in settlement of claims and

(e) non-issuance of any insurance document to customers after receipt of premium.

An Ombudsman's powers are restricted to insurance contracts of value not exceeding Rs 20 lakh (Rs 2 million). The insurance companies are required to honour the awards passed by an insurance Ombudsman within three months. Ombudsmen are appointed basically to address public grievances. Hence, the general public has an authority for addressing their issues. As this authority is appointed by the government, they have enough powers vested in them to resolve issues effectively. You can learn more about Ombudsmen, by talking to the officials of the company with whom you have a grievance. As always, you need to make sure that you have everything in place in terms of records of complaints and the basic steps you have taken in getting the issue resolved.

MAIN FEATURES OF LOKPAL AND LOKAYUKTAS ACT, 2013

The historic Lokpal and Lokayuktas Bill, 2013 was passed by Indian Parliament paving the way for establishment of an LOKPAL (Ombudsman) to fight corruption in public offices and ensure accountability on the part of public officials, including the Prime Minister, but with some safeguards.

Composition

Lokpal will consist of a chairperson and a maximum of eight members, of which 50% will be judicial members 50% members of Lokpal shall be from SC/ST/OBCs, minorities and women. Selection of chairperson and members of Lokpal through a selection committee consisting of PM, Speaker of Lok Sabha, leader of opposition in Lok Sabha, Chief Justice of India or a sitting Supreme Court judge nominated by CJI. Eminent jurist to be nominated by President of India on basis of recommendations of the first four members of the selection committee "through consensus". Lokpal's jurisdiction will cover all categories of public servants. All entities (NGOs) receiving donations from foreign source in the context of the Foreign Contribution Regulation Act (FCRA) in excess of Rs 10 lakh per year are under the jurisdiction of Lokpal Centre will send Lokpal bill to states as a model bill, states have to set up Lokayuktas through a state law within 365 days.

Powers and Functions

- Prime Minister has been brought under the purview of the Lokpal.
- Lokpal will have power of superintendence and direction over any central investigation agency including CBI for cases referred to them by the ombudsman.
- A high-powered committee chaired by the PM will recommend selection of CBI director. The collegium will comprise PM, leader of opposition in Lok Sabha and Chief Justice of India PM has been brought under purview of the Lokpal, so also central ministers and senior officials.
- Directorate of prosecution will be under overall control of CBI director. At present, it comes under law ministry.
- Appointment of director of prosecution to be based on recommendation of the Central Vigilance Commission.
- Director of prosecution will also have a fixed tenure of two years like CBI chief.
- Transfer of CBI officers investigating cases referred by Lokpal with the approval of watchdog.
- Bill incorporates provisions for attachment and confiscation of property acquired by corrupt means, even while prosecution is pending.
- Bill lays down clear timelines for preliminary enquiry and investigation and trial. Provides for special courts Public servants

will not present their view before preliminary enquiry if the case requires 'element of surprise' like raids and searches.

- Bill grants powers to Lokpal to sanction prosecution against public servants.
- CBI may appoint a panel of advocates with approval of Lokpal, CBI will not have to depend on govt advocates
- Lokpal's jurisdiction will cover all categories of public servants.
- All entities receiving donations from foreign source in the context of the Foreign Contribution Regulation Act (FCRA) in excess of Rs 10 lakh per year are brought under the jurisdiction of Lokpal.
- Provides adequate protection for honest and upright public servants.
- Lokpal will have power of superintendence and direction over any investigation agency including CBI for cases referred to them by Lokpal.
- A high powered committee chaired by the Prime Minister will recommend selection of the Director, CBI.
- Directorate of Prosecution headed by a Director of Prosecution under the overall control of Director.
- The appointment of the Director of Prosecution, CBI on the recommendation of the Central Vigilance Commission.
- Transfer of officers of CBI investigating cases referred by Lokpal with the approval of Lokpal.
- The bill also incorporates provisions for attachment and confiscation of property acquired by corrupt means, even while prosecution is pending.
- The bill lays down clear time lines for preliminary enquiry and investigation and trial and towards this end, the bill provides for setting up of special courts.
- A mandate for setting up of the institution of Lokayukta through enactment of a law by the State Legislature within a period of 365 days from the date of commencement of the Act.

E-GOVERNANCE

e-Governance or 'electronic governance' is basically the application of Information and communications Technology to the processes of Government functioning in order to bring about 'Simple, Moral, Accountable, Responsive and Transparent' (SMART) governance. This would generally involve the use of ITs by government agencies for any or all of the following reasons:

(a) Exchange of information with citizens, businesses or other government departments

(b) Speedier and more efficient delivery of public services

(c) Improving internal efficiency

(d) Reducing costs/increasing revenue

(e) Re-structuring of administrative processes and

(f) Improving quality of services.

DEFINING E-GOVERNANCE

Although the term 'e-Governance' has gained currency in recent years, there is no standard definition of this term. Different governments and organizations define this term to suit their own aims and objectives. Sometimes, the term 'e-government' is also used instead of 'e-Governance'. Some widely used definitions are listed below:

According to the ***World Bank***,

"E-Government refers to the use by government agencies of information technologies (such as Wide Area Networks, the Internet, and mobile computing) that have the ability to transform relations with citizens, businesses, and other arms of government. These technologies can serve a variety of different ends: better delivery of government services to citizens, improved interactions with business and industry, citizen empowerment through access to information, or more efficient government management. The resulting benefits can be less corruption, increased transparency, greater convenience, revenue growth, and/or cost reductions."Thus, the stress here is on use of information technologies in improving citizen-government interactions, cost-cutting and generation of revenue and transparency.

***UNESCO* defines e-Governance as:**

"Governance refers to the exercise of political, economic and administrative authority in the management of a country's affairs, including citizens' articulation of their interests and exercise of their legal rights and obligations. E-Governance may be understood as the performance of this governance via the electronic medium in order to facilitate an efficient, speedy and transparent process of disseminating information to the public, and other agencies, and for performing government administration activities." This definition visualizes the use of the electronic medium in the exercise of authority in the management of a country's affairs along with articulation of citizens' interests leading to greater transparency and efficiency.

The ***Council of Europe*** has taken e-Governance to mean:

"the use of electronic technologies in three areas of public action:-relations between the public authorities and civil society -functioning of the public authorities at all stages of the democratic process (electronic democracy) -the provision of public services (electronic public services)"In this case, the focus is on making use of electronic technologies with a view to encourage better interaction between government and citizens, promote democracy and provide public services.

The ***US E-Government Act of 2002*** defines "electronic Government" to mean (Section 3601):

"the use by the Government of web-based Internet applications and other information technologies, combined with processes that implement these technologies, to- (A) enhance the access to and delivery of Government information and services to the public, other agencies, and other Government entities; or (B)bring about improvements in Government operations that may include effectiveness, efficiency, service quality, or transformation".This definition reflects the strategy of the US

Government regarding the use of IcT in improving Government operations on the one hand and enhancing the access and delivery of information and services to citizens and government entities on the other.

Several dimensions and factors influence the definition of **e-governance** or **electronic governance**. The word "electronic" in the term e-governance implies technology driven governance. E-governance is the application of information and communication technology (ICT) for delivering government services, exchange of information communication transactions, integration of various stand-alone systems and services between government-to-citizens (G2C), government-to-business (G2B), government-to-government (G2G) as well as back office processes and interactions within the entire government framework. Through e-governance, government services will be made available to citizens in a convenient, efficient and transparent manner. The three main target groups that can be distinguished in governance concepts are government, citizens and businesses/interest groups. In e-governance there are no distinct boundaries.

Generally four basic models are available – government to customer (citizen), government to employees, government to government and government to business.

STAGES OF E-GOVERNANCE

It is evident that e-Governance is intrinsically linked with the development of computer technology, networking of computers and communication systems. In developing countries, such technologies and systems became available with a perceptible time lag as compared to developed nations. However, in the case of India, with the liberalization of the economy from the early 1990s onwards, there has been a convergence in the availability of cutting edge technologies and opportunities in the field of eGovernance. Generally speaking, the Indian experience demonstrates that the onset of e-Governance proceeded through the following phases:

(a) Computerisation:

In the first phase, with the availability of personal computers, a large number of Government offices got equipped with computers. The use of computers began with word processing, quickly followed by data processing.

(b) Networking:

In this phase, some units of a few government organizations got connected through a hub leading to sharing of information and flow of data between different government entities.

(c) On-line Presence:

With increasing internet connectivity, a need was felt for maintaining a presence on the web. This resulted in maintenance of websites by government departments and other entities. Generally, these web pages/web-sites contained information about the organizational structure, contact details, reports and publications, objectives and vision statements of the respective government entities

(d) On-line Interactivity:

A natural consequence of on-line presence was opening up of communication channels between government entities and the citizens, civil society organizations etc. The main aim at this stage was to minimize the scope of personal interface with government entities by providing downloadable Forms, Instructions, Acts, Rules etc. In some cases, this has already led to on-line submission of Forms. Most citizen-government transactions have the potential of being put on e-Governance mode.

TYPES OF INTERACTIONS IN E-GOVERNANCE

e-Governance facilitates interaction between different stake holders in governance. These interactions may be described as follows:

G2G (Government to Government):

In this case, Information and communications Technology

is used not only to restructure the governmental processes involved in the functioning of government entities but also to increase the flow of information and services within and between different entities. This kind of interaction is only within the sphere of government and can be both horizontal i.e. between different government agencies as well as between different functional areas within an organisation, or vertical i.e. between national, provincial and local government agencies as well as between different levels within an organisation. The primary objective is to increase efficiency, performance and output.

G2C (Government to Citizens):

In this case, an interface is created between the government and citizens which enables the citizens to benefit from efficient delivery of a large range of public services. This expands the availability and accessibility of public services on the one hand and improves the quality of services on the other.

It gives citizens the choice of when to interact with the government (e.g. 24 hours a day, 7 days a week), from where to interact with the government (e.g. service centre, unattended kiosk or from one'shome/workplace) and how to interact with the government (e.g. through internet, fax, telephone, email, face-to-face, etc). The primary purpose is to make government, citizen-friendly.

G2B (Government to Business):

Here, e-Governance tools are used to aid the business community – providers of goods and services – to seamlessly interact with the government. The objective is to cut red tape, save time, reduce operational costs and to create a more transparent business environment when dealing with the government. The G2binitiatives can be transactional, such as in licensing, permits, procurement and revenue collection. They can also be promotional and facilitative, such as in trade, tourism and investment. These measures help to provide a congenial environment to businesses to enable them to perform more efficiently.

G2E (Government to Employees):

Government is by far the biggest employer and like any organisation, it has to interact with its employees on a regular basis. This interaction is a two-way process between the organisation and the employee. Use of IcT tools helps in making these interactions fast and efficient on the one hand and increase satisfaction levels of employees on the other.

BENEFITS OF E-GOVERNANCE

In the end, e-Governance is about reform in governance, facilitated by the creative use of Information and communications Technology. It is expected that this would lead to:

(i) Better access to information and quality services for citizens:

IcT would make available timely and reliable information on various aspects of governance. In the initial phase, information would be made available with respect to simple aspects of governance such as forms, laws, rules, procedures etc later extending to detailed information including reports (including performance reports), public database, decision making processes etc. As regards services, there would be an immediate impact in terms of savings in time, effort and money, resulting from online and one-point accessibility of public services backed up by automation of back end processes. The ultimate objective of e-Governance is to reach out to citizens by adopting a life-cycle approach i.e. providing public services to citizens which would be required right from birth to death.

(ii) Simplicity, efficiency and accountability in the government:

Application of IcT to governance combined with detailed business process reengineering would lead to simplification of complicated processes, weeding out of redundant processes, simplification in structures and changes in statutes and regulations. The end result would be simplification of the functioning of government, enhanced decision making abilities and increased efficiency across government – all contributing to an overall environment of a more accountable government machinery. This, in turn, would result in enhanced productivity and efficiency in all sectors.

(iii) Expanded reach of governance:

Rapid growth of communications technology and its adoption in governance would help in bringing government machinery to the doorsteps of the citizens. Expansion of telephone network, rapid strides in

mobile telephony, spread of internet and strengthening of other communications infrastructure would facilitate delivery of a large number of services provided by the government. This enhancement of the reach of government – both spatial and demographic – would also enable better participation of citizens in the process of governance.

E-GOVERNANCE IN INDIA:

Government of India has been aspiring for establishing e-Governance in order to fasten the speed of the process of governance along with increased transparency. There are following initiatives taken with this regard:

e-Office- As per Cabinet approval of May 2006 the DARPG has also been made the Central Line Department for implementation of e- Office Mission Mode Project. Under the National e –Governance Plan (NeGP), which has jointly been formulated by the Department of Electronics and Information Technology (Deity) and DAR&PG, there are 27 (now 31) Mission Mode Projects. e-Office is one of the MMPs.

National Conference on e-Governance- In India every year since 1997 National Conference on e-Governance in collaboration with the Department of Information Technology and one of the state Governments is organized. The Conference offers a useful mechanism to improve cooperation amongst different levels of Government. The 16th National Conference on e- Governance based on the theme " Towards an Open Government" was held in Jaipur in February 2013. National awards are also given to government organizations, for promoting excellence in e-Governance, in seven categories.

Succinctly, if all the above mentioned institutional mechanism s work effectively the menace of corruption and policy paralysis can be controlled to a large extent. It is neither impossible nor difficult to witness these mechanisms working effectively in India as we have the institutions like Election Commission in our country which has overcome all the barrier.

REFERENCES:

1. Babu, D. R. Satish (2009). "Conceptualising the Process of E-governance: The E-Seva Experience in Hyderabad", *The Indian Journal of Public Administration*, Vol.LV, No.2, April-June. pp 165-186.
2. "Citizen Centric Administration: the Heart of Governance", *Twelfth Report of the Second Administrative Reforms Commission*, Government of India, New Delhi, 2009, pp. 8-24.
3. Dhaka, Rajvir S. (2009). "Right to Information Act and Good Governance: Operational Problems and Road Ahead", *The Indian Journal of Public Administration*, Vol.LV, No.3, July-September, pp 534-561.
4. Shamshad, Ahmad (2009). "Right to Information: Issues of Administrative Efficiency, Public Accountability and Good Governance in India", *The Indian Journal of Public Administration*, Vol.LV, No.3, July-September, pp. 562-577.
5. Paul, Samuel (2008). "India's Citizen's Charters: In Search of a Champion", *Economic and Political Weekly*, Vol. 43, No. 7 (Feburary 16-22), pp. 67-73.
6. Publication Division, MoIB, India 2014, Government of India.

Internet Sources:

1. http://goicharters.nic.in/ccinitiative.htm
2. http://www.transparencyindia.org/citizens_charters.php
3. http://www.preservearticles.com/2012022923919/what-are-the-rights-of-consumers.html

4. http://www.arc.gov.in/11threp/ARC_11thReport_Ch2.pdf
5. http://www.iimahd.ernet.in/egov/documents/opportunities-and-challenges-in-egovernance.pdf
6. http://www.it.iitb.ac.in/~prathabk/egovernance/egov.html
7. http://www.unescap.org/pdd/prs/ProjectActivities/Ongoing/gg/governance.asp

BIBLIOGRAPHY

Printed Materials

Babu, D. R. Satish (2009). "Conceptualising the Process of E-governance: The E-Seva Experience in Hyderabad", The Indian Journal of Public Administration, Vol.LV, No.2. April-June. pp 165-186.

C. Chakrapaniand Arup Mitra(1995)."Rural to Urban Migration: Access to Employment Incidence of Poverty and Determinants of Mobility", Indian Journal of Social Work, Vol. 54, No.3, July, pp.377-86.

"Citizen Centric Administration: the Heart of Governance", Twelfth Report of the Second Administrative Reforms Commission, Government of India, New Delhi, 2009, pp. 8-24.

Dhaka, Rajvir S. (2009). "Right to Information Act and Good Governance: Operational Problems and Road Ahead", The Indian Journal of Public Administration, Vol.LV, No.3. July-September. pp 534-561.

Dutta, R.K.(2000). "Policing the New millennium", Indian Police Journal, Vol. 47, Nos. 2 & 3, April-Sept 2000, pp. 58-63

Jain, Abhishek and Aaruhi Jain (2009). "Promoting Right to Information through E-Governance: A Case of E-Soochna and Other Initiatives in H.P.", The Indian Journal of Public Administration, Vol.LV, No.1. January-March. pp 36-51.

L. Radhakrishnan and K Ravi Kumar (2013). "Land Acquisition in India: Need for a Paradigm Shift" Kurukshetra [Ministry of Rural Development], Vol.61, No.5, March. Pp.30-37.

M. Lingaraju and Johnson Samuel (2005). "Rural-Urban Linkages: Does Impermanent Migration to Cities help the Rural Poor?, Nagarlok, Vol.37, No.1, Jan-March, pp.9-20.

Mishra, O.P. (2006). "Policing in the 21st Century: Areas for Concern", Indian Police Journal, Vol. 53, No. 1, (Jan-March), pp. 7-11.

Nanda, Ved P. (2006). "The 'Good Governance' Concept Revisited", Annals of the American Academy of Political and Social Science, Vol. 603, Law, Society, and Democracy: Comparative Perspectives (January), pp. 269-283.

Pattanaik, B. K. and Madan Mohan Singh (2010). "Sarva Shiksha Abhiyan and Inclusive Education', Kurukshetra [Ministry of Rural Development], Vol.58, No.11, September. Pp. 6-9.

Paul, Samuel (2008). "India's Citizen's Charters: In Search of a Champion", Economic and Political Weekly, Vol. 43, No. 7 (February 16-22), pp. 67-73.

Roy, Anupama, (2005). "The Nation and its Constitution: The Text and Context of Citizenship" in Gendered Citizenship: Historical and Conceptual Explorations, Orient Longman, Delhi.

Roy, Jaytilak Guha (2009). "The Right to Information: Some Emerging Issues of Public Concern", The Indian Journal of Public Administration, Vol.LV, No.3. July-September. pp 406-412.

Shamshad, Ahmad (2009). "Right to Information: Issues of Administrative Efficiency, Public Accountability and Good Governance in India", The Indian Journal of Public Administration, Vol.LV, No.3. July-September. pp 562-577.

Sharma, Brij Kishore (2012), Introduction to the Constitution of India, PHI Learning (Pvt) Ltd, New Delhi. (Hindi edition is also available).

Siwach, Raj Kumar and Sunil Kumar (2009). "Implementing NREGS in Haryana: A Study of Social Audit", Kurukshetra [Ministry of Rural Development], Vol.57, No.6, April. pp.41-44.

Swamy, Raju Narayana (2013). "Social Legislation and Social Security: A Case Study of MGNREGA", Kurukshetra [Ministry of Rural Development], Vol.61, No.4, February. Pp 33-40.

"What is a Social Audit", Kurukshetra [Ministry of Rural Development], Vol.57, No.6, April 2009. p.40.

Web Sources:

A note on Good Governance: http://www.img.kerala.gov.in/docs/downloads/gg.pdf

Citizen Charter: An Indian Experience: http://www.goicharters.nic.in/ccinitiative.htm

Good Governance: Origin, Concepts and Components by NayanaRenukumar: www.slideshare.net/nayanarenu/good-governance-6268274

Grievance Redressal in Bihar: http://india.gov.in/check-details-grievance-petition-bihar

Good Governance: An Overview: http://www.ifad.org/gbdocs/eb/67/e/EB-99-67-INF-4.pdf

Good Governance and Human Rights: http://www.ohchr.org/EN/Issues/Development/GoodGovernance/Pages/GoodGovernanceIndex.aspx

HimanchalPradesh: http://admis.hp.nic.in/esamadhan/Citizen/SubmitGrievance.aspx

Impact of Mobile Technology on Government: http://www.mgovservice.ru/upload/uploadfiles/Impact%20of%20Mobile%20Technologies%20on%20Government.pdf

Orissa:http://sanjoghelpline.in/website/RegistrationOnline_RWSS.aspx?SchemeId=9&srcPage=gen

Social Audit: http://www.nregs.kerala.gov.in/index.php/social-audit

Social Audit by Kurien Thomas: http://www.idgnet.org/pdfs/social%20audit.pdf

Towards Good Governance: http://reform.gov.bb/page/GOOD_GOVERNANCE.pdf

What is Good Governance?: http://www.unescap.org/pdd/prs/ProjectActivities/Ongoing/gg/governance.asp

INDEX